Stewards of God's Mysteries

Priestly Spirituality in a Changing Church

Paul J. Philibert, O.P.

This study was produced by
Melvin C. Blanchette, S.S., Daniel E. Danielson,
and Paul J. Philibert, O.P. (writer and editor)

LITURGICAL PRESS
Collegeville, Minnesota

www.litpress.org

Cover design by David Manahan, O.S.B. Photo by Corbis Photos.

Interior photos: W. P. Wittman Limited (pp. xii, 20, 30, 46, 62), Gene Plaisted (p. 6), National Federation of Priests' Councils (p. 80).

1   2   3   4   5   6   7   8

Library of Congress Cataloging-in-Publication Data

Philibert, Paul J.
    Stewards of God's mysteries : priestly spirituality in a changing church / Paul J. Philibert ... [with] Melvin C. Blanchette, Daniel E. Danielson.
        p.   cm.
    ISBN 0-8146-2976-8 (alk. paper)
    1. Priests—Religious life.   2. Spirituality—Catholic Church.   3. Catholic Church—Clergy—Religious life.   I. Blanchette, Melvin.   II. Danielson, Daniel E.   III. National Federation of Priests' Councils.   IV. Title.

BX1912.5.P49   2004
262'.14273—dc22   2003016732

Contents

Abbreviations

CL	*Christifideles Laici,* Pope John Paul II, 1988
CST	*A Century of Social Teaching,* National Conference of Catholic Bishops
DV	*Dominum et vivificantem,* Pope John Paul II, 1986
EA	*Ecclesia in America,* Pope John Paul II, 1997
EN	*Evangelii Nuntiandi,* Pope Paul VI, 1975
FIYH	*Fulfilled in Your Hearing: The Homily in the Sunday Assembly,* National Conference of Catholic Bishops, 1982
GFT	*Gather Faithfully Together: Guide for Sunday Mass,* a pastoral letter of Cardinal Roger Mahony, Archbishop of Los Angeles, Liturgy Training Publications, 1997
GMD	*Go and Make Disciples: A National Plan and Strategy for Evangelization in the United States,* National Conference of Catholic Bishops, 1992
GS	*Gaudium et Spes* (Pastoral Constitution on the Church in the Modern World), Vatican II
LEM	*Lay Ecclesial Ministry: The State of the Question,* National Conference of Catholic Bishops, 1999
LG	*Lumen Gentium* (Dogmatic Constitution on the Church), Vatican II
MCW	*Music in Catholic Worship,* National Conference of Catholic Bishops, 1973
NMI	*Novo Millennio Ineunte,* Pope John Paul II, 1999
OHB	*Our Hearts Were Burning within Us: A Pastoral Plan for Adult Faith Formation in the United States,* United States Catholic Conference, 1999
OFP	*The Basic Plan for the Ongoing Formation of Priests,* National Conference of Catholic Bishops, 2001
PDV	*Pastores Dabo Vobis,* Pope John Paul II, 1992
PO	*Presbyterorum Ordinis* (Decree on the Ministry and Life of Priests), Vatican II
RM	*Redemptoris Missio,* Pope John Paul II, 1990
SC	*Sacrosanctum Concilium* (Constitution on the Sacred Liturgy), Vatican II
SR	*The Spiritual Renewal of the American Priesthood,* United States Catholic Conference, 1973
VC	*Vita Consecrata,* Pope John Paul II, 1996
WS	*Welcoming the Stranger among Us: Unity in Diversity,* National Conference of Catholic Bishops, 2000

Foreword

The National Federation of Priests' Councils is pleased to present this small book on the spirituality of the American priest. This collaborative effort that brought together theologians, sociologists, psychologists, and pastors is an attempt to assist the priests of the United States in pursuing a spirituality that will sustain their priestly lives in the present day.

A diocesan priest-pastor, a Sulpician priest-director of an ongoing formation program for clergy, and a Dominican priest-theologian joined together to give us this work. Occasioned by the thirtieth anniversary of a document entitled *The Spiritual Renewal of the American Priesthood,* this new work, *Stewards of God's Mysteries,* is faithful to the intent of the Spiritual Renewal Task Force that set out to move from the "what" to the "how" of contemporary priestly spirituality.

The National Federation of Priests' Councils thanks all who participated in the planning phase that included three colloquia which addressed the sociological and psychological perspectives on the priesthood, theological perspectives on the life and ministry of priests, and the spirituality and mission of diocesan and religious priests.

In particular, I want to extend our thanks to Fr. Paul Philibert, O.P., Fr. Dan Danielson, and Fr. Mel Blanchette, S.S., for their dedication and commitment to this project. The ideas presented are the fruits of their reflection on the mystery of priestly life. We are indebted to them for this gift to their brother priests.

Rev. Robert J. Silva
President
National Federation of Priests' Councils

Acknowledgments

Stewards of God's Mysteries was the brainchild of the former executive director of the National Federation of Priests' Councils (NFPC), Br. Bernard F. Stratman, S.M., who is now executive director of the seminary department of the National Catholic Educational Association. Conscious of the significance of the 1973 publication, *The Spiritual Renewal of the American Priesthood,* and eager to take advantage of its thirtieth anniversary as a teachable moment, he organized this project, sought funding for it, and received the support of the NFPC president, Rev. Don Wolf. His successor as president of NFPC, Rev. Robert Silva, has not only kept a vigil over the development of this study, but has contributed the foreword to this volume.

The members of the writing committee that produced this study have been Rev. Melvin C. Blanchette, S.S., Rev. Daniel E. Danielson, and Rev. Paul J. Philibert, O.P., who served as writer and editor.

Rev. Melvin C. Blanchette, S.S., is a priest of the Society of St. Sulpice and currently the director of the Vatican II Institute of St. Patrick's Seminary in Menlo Park, California. He previously chaired the Pastoral Counseling Department of Loyola College in Columbia, Maryland, where he coordinated the doctoral studies program. He is coeditor of *Pastoral Counseling* and *The Art of Clinical Supervision: A Pastoral Counseling Perspective,* and *Grace Under Pressure.* He has written many articles dealing with priestly formation and spirituality. In 2001 he received the Pope John XXIII Award from the National Organization for Continuing Education of Roman Catholic Clergy (NOCERCC) for his contributions to the continuing formation of priests and religious.

Rev. Daniel E. Danielson is pastor of the Catholic Community of Pleasanton, California (St. Augustine Church, St. Elizabeth Seton Church). He has been a parochial pastor for twenty-five years. He is one of the founding organizers of NOCERCC. He was the founder of the Vatican II Institute for Clergy Formation in Menlo Park, California. He was also part of the writing team of the 1973 document, *The Spiritual Renewal of the American Priesthood.* For forty years he has been involved with the Jesus-Caritas Fraternity of Priests. He is a noted retreat director for priests.

Rev. Paul J. Philibert, O.P., is a friar of the Southern Dominican Province in the United States. He has taught theology at the Catholic

University of America, the Dominican School of Philosophy and Theology in Berkeley, California, and has served as director of the Institute for Church Life at the University of Notre Dame. More recently, he has been Distinguished Visiting Professor of Church and Society at Aquinas Institute of Theology in St. Louis, Missouri. In 2001, he was honored by the Center for Applied Research in the Apostolate at Georgetown University with its Cardinal Cushing Medal for longtime support of religious research. He has written widely on religious development and spirituality.

We gladly acknowledge the inspiration and contribution of the writing team for the 1973 study, *The Spiritual Renewal of the American Priesthood*. In particular we offer our thanks to Rev. Gerard T. Broccolo and Rev. Ernest F. Larkin, O Carm., who wrote and edited this still marvelous essay on priestly spirituality.

A number of colleagues and friends have offered us the benefit of their critical reading of our study as it developed. Special thanks are owed to Most Rev. Robert Morneau, bishop of the Diocese of Green Bay, to Rev. Stephen DeLeers of St. Francis Seminary in Milwaukee, Wisconsin, and Rev. Paul Minihan of the Diocese of Oakland, who provided valuable suggestions for the development of our writing.

We wish to express a particular debt of thanks to Dr. Dean R. Hoge, director of the Life Cycle Institute of the Catholic University of America, whose research and publications have provided critically important context for our own work. Dr. Hoge shared with us the protocols of focus group interviews with priests across the United States and also read early drafts of our work, providing us with valuable feedback. Dr. Hoge coauthored *Evolving Visions of the Priesthood* with Jacqueline E. Wenger, whom we also thank.

Dr. James W. Lewis, executive director of the Louisville Institute, helped NFPC shape a proposal that ultimately won the favor of the board of the Louisville Institute. We are deeply grateful for that support and sincerely hope that our study and its process for clergy renewal will fulfill the hopes of the Louisville Institute for our work.

In launching the project in 1998, the then NFPC president, Rev. Donald Wolf, commented: "At the end of the decade and century, the NFPC considers this occasion a unique opportunity to take a fresh look at the circumstances within which American priests live their lives and exercise their ministry today. This project is designed to enable priests and Church leaders to unpack and encourage reflection on how priests' normal, ministerial lives in the midst of American culture invite and provide opportunities for them to die to self and live joyously and confidently in God."

A number of colloquia and consultations were held in preparation for this anniversary publication. They were overseen by an NFPC-established task force, including two members of the original drafting group of the 1973 document, to update this resource for the priests of the United States today. Task force participants included: Rev. Daniel Danielson (Oakland), Rev. Amador Garza (Brownsville), Msgr. Denis Herron (Brooklyn), Rev. Dominic Maruca, S.J. (St. Mary's Seminary and University, Baltimore), Rev. Gregory Peatee (Toledo), Rev. Donald Sterling (Baltimore), Rev. Robert Silva (Stockton), and Rev. Donald Wolf (Oklahoma City). Most Rev. Richard Hanifen of Colorado Springs, as chairman of the USCCB Secretariat on Priestly Life and Ministry, helped the committee initiate the project.

Sr. Lea Woll, S.L.W., of Learning Partnerships in Chicago, and James Ivers, director of Resurrection Center in Woodstock, Illinois, assisted in the design and facilitation of the various consultation activities. Brother Bernard Stratman served as staff to the project from 1998–2002.

Major project funding was provided by Guest House, the Raskob Foundation, and Rev. Vincent Dwyer, O.C.S.O., from a fund established at the close of the Center for Human Development. We also wish to gratefully acknowledge the support for this project provided by the following Religious Institutes and members of the Conference of Major Superiors of Men:

Capuchin Franciscans, White Plains, New York

Capuchin Franciscans, St. Augustine Province

Claretians, Eastern Province

Congregation of the Holy Ghost

Crosier Fathers and Brothers

Franciscans, Holy Name Province

Franciscans, Sacred Heart Province

Glenmary Home Missioners

Maryknoll Fathers and Brothers

Oblates of Mary Immaculate

Order of Friars Minor, St. John the Baptist Province

Order of St. Augustine, Our Mother of Good Counsel Province

Order of St. Augustine, St. Thomas Province

Passionists, Holy Cross Province

Paulist Fathers

Priests of the Sacred Heart

Redemptorists, New Orleans Province

Society of Jesus, Chicago Province

Society of Jesus, Maryland Province

Society of Jesus, New Orleans Province

Society of Jesus, New York Province

Society of Jesus, Oregon Province

Marianists, Province of St. Louis

Marists, San Francisco Province

Marists, Washington Province

Society of St. Sulpice

Society of the Divine Word

Society of the Precious Blood, Kansas City Province

St. Joseph Society of the Sacred Heart

Trinitarians, Immaculate Heart of Mary Province

Vincentians, Eastern Province.

Finally, we gratefully acknowledge all priests who have ministered in the United States Church with courage and commitment during these thirty years of unprecedented change and conflict. We likewise salute the bishops of our country who have persevered in finding new formulas for dialogue and presbyteral growth and have kept their eyes on the vision and challenges of the Second Vatican Council. May they find here assistance worthy of their hopes.

Chapter One

Setting the Scene

Think of us in this way, as servants of Christ and
stewards of God's mysteries. Moreover, it is required
of stewards that they be found trustworthy. (1 Cor 4:1-2)

Paul, in establishing his authority to guide the Church at
Corinth, appeals to the claim that he is the servant of Christ
and a steward of God's mysteries. This is one of the earliest
expressions in the New Testament of the character of ecclesial leadership. It is a fitting description for ecclesial leadership today and a solid foundation for the many roles that
priests play as they follow in Paul's footsteps as evangelists
and pastors.

Priests certainly are stewards of God's mysteries. They teach
them as merciful revelation, celebrate them in the liturgy, in-
voke them as healing and pardon, and above all, live them as
the deepest meaning of their own lives. But in truth, it is one
mystery, embracing all of God's mercies, that guides priests in
their life and ministry. That is the paschal mystery of God's
Son, Jesus Christ.

It is the paschal mystery of Christ that so many priests and
bishops are experiencing in their own lives these days. In ways
they would not have imagined before the *Boston Globe* system-
atically undertook to get to the bottom of some particularly ab-
horrent cases of sexual abuse, the lives of American priests
have dramatically changed. For more than a year, newspaper
accounts of priests and bishops who compromised their commitment to celibate chastity have appeared with disheartening
frequency and spilled over into national television, radio, and
magazine journalism. Many priests know someone whose acts
of abuse or whose past indiscretions have caught up with
them, leading to their removal from ministry. Many priests fear
accusations themselves from people who might imagine that

they are reviving "repressed memories" or who might conjure up injuries from the past.

As others have noted, these years of revelations about abuse and some bishops' failures to remove perpetrators has squandered much of the moral authority of the Church and much of the goodwill usually accorded to Catholic bishops and priests by the public. Whatever their own personal record of moral rectitude and pastoral zeal, priests have suffered some chilling of relations with parishioners or acquaintances—and a retreat from contact with children and youth. A climate of suspicion hangs over the priesthood itself, despite the effective ministry and cordial generosity of the vast majority of priests.

This is one part of the context of ordained ministry today; not the only significant part at all, but surely the most notorious. The spiritual life of priests is affected, even shaped, by this and other challenges. This study undertakes to describe these challenges and to illustrate the response of faithful disciples in priestly life.

Thirty years ago, U.S. bishops and priests were preoccupied with the changes introduced into Catholic pastoral ministry by Vatican II. These issues included the growing expectations placed on priests through the multiplication of ministries in the parish, the troubled morale of priests concerned about their identity in the postconciliar context, and the discord arising from disparate reactions to the Council itself. *The Spiritual Renewal of the American Priesthood* was published by the National Conference of Catholic Bishops (NCCB) in 1973 in order to address these and other issues. Its goal was to encourage priests to discover healthy ways to address the conflicts in their lives and to interpret the pain and difficulties of their adjustment in terms of Christ's paschal mystery.

But the question of spiritual renewal has to begin with Christian spirituality itself. What is Christian spirituality, and do priests have a special version of it? We accept the following understanding of Christian spirituality that was developed in the 1973 document:

Christian spirituality consists in the living out in experience, throughout the whole course of our lives, of the death-resurrection of Christ that we have been caught up in by baptism. It consists in living out in our day and in our lives the passage from sin and darkness to the light and warmth of God's gracious love. . . .

The spiritual life is, above all, life. . . . It is the experience of the paschal mystery, the passage of the Lord Jesus to the Father, accepted and lived in faith. Where is it found? It is found in the interface of the individual Christian and American culture; in simple ministerial func-

tions, from baptizing a child to defending the right to life; in rectory life where it may be the generation gap can be spanned only by almost heroic tolerance on both sides. . . . The challenges in the priest's life, large and small, call on the priest's resources to identify himself personally with Christ's mystery. (SR 1–2)

The "paschal mystery" is theology's formula for naming the invitation given to all the baptized to follow as disciples of Christ on the path to transformed life. "O marvelous exchange!" we pray in the first antiphon for Evening Prayer I of the Octave of Christmas, "Man's Creator has become man, born of a virgin. We have been made sharers in the divinity of Christ who humbled himself to share in our humanity." We enter this divine bargain with Christ—God offers us the gift of redemption and immortality, and we offer to God our lives, our presence, and our passion for life. The Cross of Jesus and his Easter resurrection are the symbols of this paschal mystery, just as this familiar memorial acclamation summarizes its essential theology: "Dying, you destroyed our death; rising you restored our life; Lord Jesus, come in glory!"

Those things that are considered waste in the eyes of the world—suffering, loss, pain, grief, and death—become active symbols of the power of God. Christ's triumph over death in his resurrection promises meaning and hope to us in the midst of our own trials and sufferings. The logic of the paschal mystery is that the faithful, who are joined to Christ through baptism and the Holy Spirit, share in his passing over—or passing through—human loss and suffering into a graced renewal of life. By following Christ through suffering and conflict in the hope of resurrection, his disciples are purified and transformed.

It is now thirty years since the publication of *The Spiritual Renewal of the American Priesthood* by the NCCB. The National Federation of Priests' Councils (NFPC), which partnered with the NCCB in writing the 1973 document, decided a few years back to prepare a thirty-year follow-up study to assess changes in ecclesial and ministerial life and their impact on priests and their spiritual lives.

From the start of this project, we have maintained two important positions. First, we believe that the 1973 document, *The Spiritual Renewal of the American Priesthood,* is still valid in its principles and perspectives. You will see how often we have cited it in a sidebar. We hope that this new study will send readers (especially seminary professors and seminarians) back to the original text. Second, the chapters we have created here are proposed as a "study document." They are intended to become the basis for group study and dialogue between diocesan priests and their bishops, or between religious priests and their major superiors. In that sense, this is just the beginning of what we hope can become a fresh process for renewal.

THE PLAN OF THE BOOK

To resituate the work of 1973 in our present ecclesial context, we revisit in chapter 2 the topic of "The Cultural Context for Ordained Ministry Today." In chapter 3, "Christ's Priesthood Lived through the Paschal Mystery," we link the ministerial priesthood to the priesthood of all believers in order to show how the Church's emerging focus on an apostolic laity calls for strong ordained leadership. That examination of the theology of priesthood leads directly to chapter 4, "The Shape of Ordained Ministry Today," where we spell out the complementary roles that have clearly emerged for priests in recent decades.

The next two chapters are devoted to priests' human development and spiritual growth. Chapter 5, "A Lifetime of Transformation through Discipleship," follows the lead given by Pope John Paul II in spelling out the issues for human development in the course of a priest's life. Chapter 6, "Living the Practices of the Spiritual Life," leads readers through a look at spiritual practices in the life of a typical parish priest, reflecting on his need for practices and their benefits in a busy and fulfilled life. Along the way, we pay attention to the ways in which ordained ministry has evolved, particularly in terms of what we call a "comprehensive" as opposed to a purely "cultic" understanding of priesthood. We give particular attention to the means by which a priest can cultivate a robust and sustaining spiritual life despite the stresses of the present day.

In the Roman Catholic Church, priests are ordained to serve as assistants to the bishops and they depend on the bishops in the exercise of their power. The local church is urged—by Scripture, the Second Vatican Council, and papal and episcopal exhortations—to rediscover and cultivate its spiritual unity. The deepest hope of the leadership of the NFPC and of the authors is that this study will provide a realistic and useful framework for healing dialogue and effective collaboration to bring about that result.

We express our gratitude to the Louisville Institute which provided a generous grant to support the consultations with pastors, study, and writing that were required to prepare this publication. Our aim is to enhance the life and vitality of Catholic parishes and priestly ministry across the land through this assistance to Catholic bishops and priests. In this way, we trust that we will fulfill the expectations of the Louisville Institute whose mission is the revitalization of Christian congregational life in America.

Agenda for Personal and Group Reflection

Following each of the short chapters below, you will find questions and points for reflection. The aim of this process is twofold. First, *your* experience is unique, and it will be important to bring your experience to bear on the topics and issues raised here. Does this account of Catholic priesthood today match your experience? If so, how does it help you understand priesthood, confirm your call, or challenge you to deeper generosity? It will be important to make note of that for your own benefit.

Second, this book is an invitation to common study and dialogue. So you will find discussion questions for group work. These groups may be either formal or informal, official or ad hoc. But whatever group process you find possible, you will certainly derive greater benefit from common study and discussion than from individual study alone. There is a wisdom in group study and sharing that an isolated reader will not experience by himself. That is the goal of this enterprise and of this little book; the discussion questions are a resource for dialogue.

May God bless your reading and your conversation!

A Prayer before Dialogue

God of all the ages, Master of all times and cultures,
in your mercy, shed light upon our minds and hearts
as we gather as servants of Christ and stewards of your mysteries.
By your Holy Spirit, confirm us in the faith of the Church,
touch our hearts with your call to follow Jesus as evangelists and pastors,
grant us insight, courage, and love as we work and discern together
about our lives as (bishops and) priests.
We thank you for our holy calling to devote our lives
to the coming of your kingdom.
May your Church and our ministry within it always serve your loving Providence
and the kingdom of truth and justice, unity and peace
that you have promised us.
We ask this, Father, through our Lord Jesus Christ in the power of his Holy Spirit.
Amen.

Chapter Two

The Cultural Context for Ordained Ministry Today

In the thirty years since the original *Spiritual Renewal of the American Priesthood,* the formative influences upon U.S. culture have changed and multiplied. The switch from the relatively stable, homogeneous, and modern contours of the Cold War era to the flexible, heterogeneous, and postmodern fluidity of our globalized world represents a paradigm shift. The landscape of the world is changing. A future is revealing itself. Given these shifts, a never-before-seen U.S. culture is unfolding before our eyes.

Today's cultural newness provides an inescapable context for priests to experience the dying and rising of Jesus. Out of their prayer and reflection on the culture's challenges, priests of the United States must preach with their whole selves the timeless mystery of Jesus Christ. Pope John Paul II underscored this for the Church of America when he wrote, "It is necessary to inculturate preaching in such a way that the Gospel is proclaimed in the language and the culture of its hearers" (*EA* §70). The Holy Father's words exhort priests to be sensitively aware of their day-to-day environment and its emerging newness. As the future of U.S. culture is disclosed, priests will have to recognize and till the new growths within this soil.

Too often cultural shifts are viewed only negatively. The new is unknown and feared. Change is disruptive; chaos results. Not only does this concern apply to the activity and self-awareness of a nation's culture and subcultures, it also applies to the Church's culture and her various subcultures. For some of our Catholic brothers and sisters, clergy and laity alike, change is a source of discouragement and anger. Faced with so much social change, some desire the Church to be a countersign providing stability and sameness. Unquestionably, the Church of yesterday, today, and tomorrow will preach the same Jesus Christ. Yet the ways we preach and live out this saving message effectively will differ from one people to another, providing even further riches as peoples interact.

PRIESTLY DIVERSITY

"All who accept the Gospel undergo change as we continually put on the mind of Christ by rejecting sin and becoming more faithful disciples in His Church. Unless we undergo conversion, we have not truly accepted the Gospel." (*GMD* §12)

The priests of the United States represent a great diversity in theology, background, and approaches to pastoral ministry. This diversity, while seen sometimes as a blessing, can also be a source of disunity within a presbyterate or religious community. There are two related temptations here. One is to simply dismiss and refuse to be in dialogue with laity or priests who approach matters differently, and to associate only with people of like mind. The other temptation is to throw oneself into one's local ministry (functional "congregationalism"), and refuse to be involved with other priests or with anything beyond one's own narrow world. The recognition of this ambiguity represents a call to conversion.

But priests are in fact a part of a common presbyterate under the local bishop or religious superior. Their efforts to reach out to one another, to listen to one another, to find areas of common ground, and to have common pastoral initiatives really express the call of the Holy Spirit. This means dying to one's own self-sufficiency and to one's own closed points of view. But this self-sacrifice for the sake of communion also offers the powerful experience of the Resurrection discovered in priests' ministering together as brothers, in mutual appreciation and support.

These efforts to reach out can take many forms: e.g., the formation of priest support groups such as the Jesus-Caritas Fraternity of Priests or Emmaus groups or even priest-lay support groups; working on common projects together through the presbyteral council or the clergy formation functions of the diocese; or social gatherings for anniversaries, funerals, ordinations, and dedications. All of these require effort and initiative, and at times this effort can lead to frustration as those reaching out find that not all are interested in such contact or involvement. But the call of the Spirit is to reach out, not to withdraw. The effort to stay in communion with the broader Church at various levels makes great demands on the personality of the priest and calls on his virtues of hope and perseverance as much as anything else in his life.

The bishops of the United States view this ecclesial diversity at every level as a gift to the future of the nation's culture and to the Church, all the while aware that many are fearful. The spirituality that underscores their reflections on culture calls priests and the entire community of faith not to fear the death of what is known. They encourage priests to walk into the newness of a future life by rising with Jesus.

To begin this process of reflection on the context for today's ministry, it is paramount to discern and explore various phenomena of both the national and ecclesial culture. This reflection is only a first sketch. The refinement of this reflection is left to groups of priests who will help one another grow and face the challenges of today's emerging culture with hope.

"Some of our fears are tied to what we see as a defense of our own culture or way of life. Many people cling—rightfully so—to their distinctive culture. They fear a loss of their own familiar ways of doing things as they encounter new images and practices of community life and worship that are foreign to them." (*WS* §27)

THE CHANGING SHAPE OF INSTITUTIONAL LIFE

From the late nineteenth through much of the twentieth century, the citizens of the United States saw themselves less as individuals and more as members of identifying institutions. Modern institutions were structural goliaths that shaped not only business and commerce, but also social wellbeing and religious identity. The buildings that housed these institutions witnessed to their greatness. The bigger the building, the greater the institution's attractiveness. The more attractive the institution, the greater was the desire for institutional affiliation. In the end, it was clear that the external appearance of the institution was a reflection of its soul.

Today, the grand institutions that offered stability, direction, and social identity in the past are no more. Institutional disloyalty has been on the rise for many years. This shift is a result of valuing self over and above any institution. The individual takes precedence over the communal. Whereas the norm for earlier generations was to work for one institution loyally for an entire lifetime, today's Americans do not place their trust in an institution to provide them definition.

Now the individual shapes the institution. When a person's talents no longer find meaningful expression in the institution, the individual leaves the organization. Accordingly institutional loyalty is no longer of paramount importance. There has been a loss of a sense of the common good and individualism is clearly in the ascendancy. More often people now focus on themselves and the things that affect them to the exclusion of taking responsibility for the broader society of which they are a part and to which they have substantial contributions to make.

In many cases individuals have manipulated institutions for personal gain. As manipulations went public, so too did the public's growing distrust in institutions. Now it seems evident that corporate institutions of business can serve as a cover for the gain or protection of a few individuals. In this framework, the recent explosion of events—the downturn of corporate America, the partial collapse of the dot.com industry, and the public airing of the American church's mismanagement of priest personnel—finds cause.

We cannot go on without noting the effect of the reported cases of clergy abuse of minors over the last forty years. Priests are especially shocked by the cover-ups that some bishops have engaged in since the 1990s. The U.S. bishops' *Charter for the Protection of Children and Young People* has responded to institutional abuse and sin. However, the bishops' charter seems harsh to many priests, and it has left them feeling angry and abandoned, wondering if they have been sacrificed for the public relations needs of the hierarchy. While all priests are anxious to protect the young members of their flock, it is difficult for many priests to think of their bishops as fathers or brothers in light of the bishops' policy. The fear of accusation haunts many good priests today.

Priests likewise feel judged by the general public. By and large they are supported in their own parishes, but they wonder how the marginal Catholic views them: with suspicion? Caution? Some priests have become very discouraged, feeling put upon from all sides. There is certainly a call here to experience the Lord's death.

In today's postmodern climate, the Church is seen as one more questionable institution. For many, the *bella figura* of the Church (her public face) is viewed not so much as a mirror of her soul but as a pall to cover the disease of her soul. The credibility of the Church's statements can no longer be taken for granted. Priests encounter many people who are simply annoyed by any Church institution. Out-of-date traditions and practices become the object of their disappointment. The habit of secrecy in ecclesiastical decision making gives rise to suspicion of the Church's integrity.

"The church's social doctrine is a moral vision which aims to encourage governments, institutions and private organizations to shape a future consonant with the dignity of every person."
(*EA* §55)

While many priests have little or no difficulty going along with the Church's authority, some priests active in leadership and ministry take issue with the institution's management, both nationally and internationally. For the Church's institutional credibility to have a future, transparency must govern decision making on the parochial, diocesan, and universal levels of church administration. We must let go of forms of institutional governance that continue to provide food for distrust. As pastoral leaders, priests will have to be models of integrity and accountability not only for the Church but for the nation as well.

A FUTURE FOR FAMILIES

The same history that shaped these shifts in institutional values propelled changes in the understanding of family. The number of single-parent families continues to grow— and for a variety of reasons. Second marriages are common. Any hope of returning to a past era is futile. Moving consciously into this future is essential because the new reality is firmly in place. The dying and rising of Jesus must be read into the present.

Data regarding divorce among Catholics does not significantly differ from that of other people in the United States. Priestly ministry has been forced to respond to this situation. It has had a major impact on the ministries and services provided by Catholic parishes. Shifts in family dynamics have made priests more sensitive to people experiencing family breakdowns. On the other hand, many Catholics still see the Church's leadership as condemning, without sensitive appreciation of the situations that give rise to divorce. The Church's ministry to persons whose lives are affected by divorce is a symbol of the pain and anguish that so many Catholics experience living on the periphery of the Church, awaiting a word of welcome and an outstretched arm.

For priests, the compassionate word and the outstretched arm are not easy to offer. At times, priests' grappling with issues of faith and morals constricts their ability to be an image of the Good Shepherd who embraces the lost sheep. Finding balance between acting as the authentic interpreter of Church teaching in a parish setting and offering the compassionate word is a difficult journey for most. How can priests welcome all God's people and help them grow from where they are into a

"Remember we are always the Body of Christ, always in communion with one another. Know that you can ask for help from one another. Let others know that. In the simplest deeds of daily life at work or at home, be conscious of this life we share in Christ, of its joy and its hope. Do not see yourself as separate from others, but understand that we who are the Church are one with others." (*GFT* §109)

deeper union with God? This is a challenge for them to die to their own self-righteousness without sacrificing their personal integrity.

To rise and dialogue with our sisters and brothers on the margins—including those who are unreconciled Catholics; divorced and remarried persons; single parents; gay, lesbian, or bisexual persons—necessarily involves great ambiguity. Struggling to master avoidance can give rise to a priestly spirituality that fosters a community of faith and supports the members in need. The future of family life will emerge not only from the interactions of the nuclear or extended family, but also from the interaction among the various parts of the mystical body of Christ, the family that is the Church. The manner in which priests embrace those in our parish family who are in need will shape the future of the family that is the local church.

Generation X

The shifts in attitudes regarding institutions and family life just noted are most visible in the generation that followed the baby boomer generation. Often called "Generation X"—persons born between 1961 and 1983—these women and men have personally experienced the shadows of institutional mismanagement and failed family life. Their response has been a desire to deconstruct and react to so many false appearances. Gen X champions the individual's right to express himself or herself without getting bogged down in compromising institutional affiliations, whether in the family or in society.

This generation characteristically has difficulty with long-term commitments. They enter marriage, religious profession, ordination, and careers with what seems to be contractual loopholes or provisional approaches. They have their reasons for this. As this generation looks back on those who easily committed themselves in the past, they see too many cases of joyless, disgruntled lives. So typically this generation enters into commitments reluctantly, and in many cases they postpone life-orienting decisions until later in life. Unlike earlier generations, they do not rush into commitments. This can be a good thing in terms of maturity. But even when those commitments are finally made, they still tend to be more tentative and conditioned.

Many priests from this generation have to struggle to see themselves in a lifetime commitment to priestly ministry. To consciously shut off the option of leaving priestly ministry and to plunge deeply into priestly life requires a real dying to self, and it requires finding one's whole future happiness and peace in Christ and his call. This issue exists for all priests of course, but it is more acute for younger generations.

Consumer Mentality

Much of American society has developed a consumer mentality about almost everything, including religion. The idea that "religion is good for the family" is widespread, but it does not make a great deal of difference with what religion the family affiliates. For priests who have been trained in the theology of the Church that understands the Church itself as an object of faith ("You cannot have God for your Father if you do not have the Church for your mother"), this is a painful thing to observe in people's lives.

This consumer attitude tends to make priests into purveyors of services: "We offer a wonderful youth program; we have childcare for all parish events and Masses; we have vacation Bible school, etc." Many fine Catholic people will opt out of practicing the Catholic faith without a twinge of guilt or regret in order to be part of a more "contemporary" approach to worship elsewhere. Priests struggle to understand how someone can walk away from the Eucharist, which is the center of their lives. Yet, parish priests painfully witness such departures all the time.

For many in American society, religion serves a therapeutic function, not a meaning-of-life function. Religion seems to be necessary for the weak, the sick, and losers. It's a crutch for those who otherwise would not make it in society. Thus religion becomes marginalized, of secondary importance, trivialized, and very much privatized. "Each to his own God; each in his own way," becomes the societal norm.

At the same time we observe a growing attraction to "fundamentalist" churches in American society. The largest membership in these, whether new megachurches or small Bible churches, are former Catholics. These churches are particularly attractive to people who are impatient with ambiguity, who want black-and-white answers. These people are often looking for a faith that is more alive and evangelical than what they see practiced and proclaimed in more traditional Catholic churches. Furthermore, for many Hispanic immigrants from Latin America, neighborhood Pentecostal churches are closer to the size of the congregation that they knew back in their original homeland.

There are, however, some healthy challenges in all this. Priests can no longer take people's participation in the Catholic Church for granted. People have much less tolerance for being abused from the pulpit or listening week after week to uninspired or undigested homilies. They will tend to look elsewhere when meaningful lay involvement is not developed and encouraged, or when the music at worship is poor and unengaging. "Faith grows when it is well expressed in celebration. Good celebrations foster and nourish faith. Poor celebrations may weaken and destroy it" (*MCW* §6).

Good ministry in such a culture requires priests who assume a prophetic role with which many priests are uncomfortable. It calls priests to stand up against the view that this world is all there is. To discover that many people who are otherwise quite fine view the priest's role as insignificant or largely ritualistic is a challenge. As he ministers faithfully and prophetically in their midst, the priest experiences the power of the Holy Spirit in his life, and he experiences a death to the values of this world—especially to social esteem and public influence.

The Catholic Church is called to be evangelical. Evangelism is not the exclusive property of Bible churches. Pope Paul VI wrote: "the Church exists in order to evangelize. It is her deepest identity" (*EN* §14). But for the most part Catholic evangelism has not become a reality in the minds of the Catholic hierarchy, the Catholic clergy, or the Catholic people. Moving the Church in that direction—out into the marketplace—is a very challenging task for today's priests.

A hundred years ago, our Catholic history was lived in ghetto Catholicism where Catholics kept to themselves, hostile to Protestants, occupying the lowest levels of society. The fact that those days are for the most part over has not changed our self-contained stance. Outreach for both clergy and laity requires living with uncertainty and moving into an area for which priests have not been trained and in which they are not instinctively comfort-

"To celebrate the liturgy means to do the action or perform the sign in such a way that its full meaning and impact shine forth in clear and compelling fashion. Since liturgical signs are vehicles of communication and instruments of faith, they must be simple and comprehensible. Since they are directed to fellow human beings, they must be humanly attractive. They must be meaningful and appealing to the body of worshippers or they will fail to stir up faith and people will fail to worship the Father. . . . In true celebration each sign or sacramental action will be invested with the personal and prayerful faith, care, attention and enthusiasm of those who carry it out." (*MCW* §§7 & 9)

able. There is a dying to security here, but likewise a deeper trust in the power of Jesus' resurrection.

MOBILITY

Mobility continues to be a significant factor in American society, both social mobility and geographic mobility. It is difficult to develop a stable community when its membership keeps changing. Belonging to the parish may mean very little among the choices that a great number of Catholics make. Sociologists have expressed their concern that *social capital,* people's involvement in the smaller groupings of their society, has noticeably diminished in recent decades (cf. Robert Putnam, *Bowling Alone*). An appreciation for the multifaceted nature of community has lessened significantly, leading to increased individualism and disconnectedness from the broader society. Often neighborhoods are no longer real social groupings in any true sense.

And yet the Catholic faith is all about the formation of community, with God and with one another. It is as the people of God that the Church comes together in worship and reaches out to serve. But Christians are forced to do this in the face of a society that has few natural underpinnings left for such corporate activity. The busy pace of people's lives also militates against their giving time to form communities of meaning.

The easy way out for the priest is simply to try to meet each individual person's needs day by day and to try to respond to particular situations within families, without worrying about building some sort of community in which they can be mutually supportive of one another. Forming Christian community, large or small, in present day American society, is pushing uphill at considerable sacrifice with frequent frustrations. Further, in most areas of the country, the Catholic population is ethnically diverse. This is particularly true along the coasts. This also complicates community building.

While there are some priests who can minister to the ethnic communities using their native language and culture, many times priests who are not native to the population are called upon to minister to a people whose culture and language they grasp only marginally. This is true in parallel fashion of priests from other cultures who are called upon to minister to Anglo or Asian communities.

"Whether we notice it or not, we are surrounded by the indifferent and unbelievers. Some of them used to believe, others never did, still more don't even know what we believe. But all of them are our neighbors. Being in their midst places us in a missionary predicament—one we didn't choose and which catches us off guard. But as a consequence, our Christian life has to become what we know its true nature really is: apostolic. The problem is, not only are we not ready for apostolic action, we were prepared for a Christian life where there is no room for apostolic action. Not only have we not been formed to be apostolic, we have been deformed to think that apostolic action has nothing to do with us." (Delbrêl 1980, 199)

"The Church in America must be a vigilant advocate, defending against any unjust restriction of the natural right of individual persons to move freely within their own nation and from one nation to another. Attention must be called to the rights of migrants and their families and to the respect for their human dignity, even in cases of non-legal immigration." (*EA* §65)

"Communion must be cultivated and extended day by day at every level in the structures of each church's life. There, relations between bishops, priests and deacons, between pastors and the entire people of God . . . must all be clearly characterized by communion." (*NMI* §45)

In both cases, many priests feel that they are not adequate to the task or that they do not know with confidence how to do good ministry in another culture.

"All cultures are in a constant process of change as their members seek new ways to address individual and group needs and as they encounter new situations and other cultures. Indeed, no culture is either permanent or perfect. All constantly need to be evangelized and uplifted by the good news of Jesus Christ." (*WS* 28)

They fear making insensitive remarks or judging something in another culture by the standards of their own culture. They are awkward and therefore have a tendency to shy away from ministry with and for these people. They struggle to make the parish one unified community, where different ethnic groups enrich rather than negate the community's development. They try to make sure that there is a place for all, so that no one group is treated with discrimination and given the worst places and the worst times for their celebrations and events. As priests struggle to address all these complexities of culture, they need a positive outlook on change.

Here again priests are called on to reach out beyond their instinctive comfort zone, even though this may be awkward for them. Generally the people for whom they make this effort see beneath their struggles and their awkwardness, and these people rally around them with gratitude. In such moments of generous communion priests can experience the love that flows from service, the gift of the risen Lord alive in the midst of the community of faith.

Overwork and the Priest Shortage

We have not yet mentioned the shortage of priests and its toll upon the energies and morale of bishops and their ordained helpers. Beginning in the middle 1980s, Richard Schoenherr and his associates began to study the demographics of priesthood recruitment and retention in the U.S. In 1994, Schoenherr's data predicted a forty percent decline in the number of diocesan priests over a forty year period stretching from 1966 to 2006. Many Catholic bishops were slow to pay attention to his data, and some others simply rejected his study. But the impact of a decline roughly comparable to Schoenherr's projections is now incontestable. The results of this change are being felt by the many priests across the country who are being asked to supply for the loss of numbers in the diocesan clergy by assuming pastoral leadership for a plurality of parishes. Priests so overextended feel the pain of letting down parishioners who want (and expect) more time and attention from their pastors than they are able to give.

Many find parish hopping to be an exhausting exercise and ultimately less fulfilling than being a resident pastor who is genuinely rooted in a single parish community.

Many priests are experiencing exhaustion and frustration simply because they are being asked to do much too much. Often they assume these multiple leadership positions without any special preparation or without clear understandings—on both sides—of how they are to relate to the local lay or religious overseer of the mission parish. Ambiguity about the priest's true role in such situations and conflicting expectations about his priorities for pastoral action is a painful fact of life for many priests. Priests experience real suffering here. They are frustrated because they cannot do what they had hoped to do with their lives. They are also hurt by the disappointment of those whom they are making heroic efforts to serve.

Yet this is a call to enter into a ministry with and through others, enabling their charisms and gifts for the people of God. This requires sacrifice and an acknowledgment that the priest does not have all the gifts. However, there also is a profound experience of the power of the Resurrection in seeing the Holy Spirit as the source of the myriad gifts given to competent laity in the Church in our day.

Because priests can no longer "do it all," if they ever could, priests now have to prioritize their work more than ever. That means letting some things go, perhaps some cherished things. There is a diminishment, a dying here too.

CONCLUSION

This does not pretend to be an adequate overview of U.S. culture today nor of the Catholic Church within that culture. These are merely suggestive topics and highlights offered to bishops and priests to help them flesh out, in company with others, the meaning of their own experiences and insights.

Priests do not minister in a theoretical world but in the real world of American society in the twenty-first century. A priest's spirituality is not found in a theoretical world either. It is lived out in the challenges and joys of daily living, and in serving the people entrusted to his care. Priests enter more deeply into the dying and rising of Jesus as they accept their experience of ministry and

"Sensing the paschal mystery being revealed in his society, [the priest] is pained and at the same time he rejoices; he is challenged, yet he believes; he is inspired, yet humiliated; he is tossed between hope and despair, between riches and poverty, between acceptance and rejection, between relevancy and what is irrelevant; he is inspirited and dispirited. He is drawn further to reflect upon himself and discern this same mystery active in his work, his relationships and his prayerful search for God." (SR 9)

the challenges and joys embodied in American culture itself as a call to live Christ's paschal mystery today. Their call to holiness comes from their fellow priests, from the people of their parish, from the authorities in the Church, and from trying to bring the vision of the Gospel to bear on all of these.

The spiritual life of priests is lived out in this context and it can be enriched and deepened by these challenges, but only to the extent that priests are reflective enough and prayerful enough to discern the call of the Lord in the midst of everything that fills their days. We turn next to a description of the priest's call, examining ordained ministerial priesthood in the wider context of Christ's priesthood and of the participation of all the faithful in that mystery.

Agenda for Personal and Group Reflection

QUESTIONS FOR THE INDIVIDUAL PRIEST

1. Where do you locate yourself in the changing U.S. culture? Are you hopeful or discouraged by the complexity of our circumstances?

2. Are you linked to a support group, study group, or common project with other priests or ministers?

3. Has the widespread feeling of mistrust of institutions had some effect on your own attitudes toward your diocese and the Church?

4. Do you feel caught between the Church's official teaching on moral issues and your own desires to help people in messy moral predicaments?

5. Is Christ's call definitive for you? Is your commitment to priesthood a source of energy for you?

6. What are the one or two greatest challenges that the postmodern situation creates for your ministry as a priest?

7. Where does your ministry call you beyond your comfort zone?

QUESTIONS FOR GROUP DISCUSSION

1. Should there be a legitimate pluralism of attitudes toward the Church's predicament today? Why do some priests relish diversity and others find it painful and dangerous?

2. How has the bishops' *Charter for the Protection of Children and Young Persons* been received within your circle of priests? What questions about it do you want to bring to your own bishop or major superior?

3. What are issues that need to be aired among your priests (with the bishop or major superior) relative to the credibility of the Church's teachings, especially in moral matters?

4. How can priests help one another to recommit themselves more deeply to their call to priesthood?

5. What are the one or two greatest challenges that the postmodern situation creates for you as priests?

6. How is the priest shortage affecting your diocese? Have you discussed the shortage and its consequences as a presbyterate? What does the future hold for your diocese in terms of utilizing permanent deacons or nonordained personnel for parish administration?

Chapter Three

Christ's Priesthood Lived through the Paschal Mystery

THREE MEANINGS OF PRIESTHOOD

There are three meanings of priesthood in Catholic theology, and all three need to be understood in terms of one another. The first meaning is the priesthood of Jesus Christ who is our mediator with God and who offers our lives of faith and service to God as the living sacrifice of the Church along with his own eternal sacrifice. The second meaning of priesthood is the common priesthood of the faithful who have become a priestly people (1 Pet 2:5) and who offer their sanctified lives to God in everything that they do. The third meaning of priesthood is the ordained ministerial service of bishops and priests who are ordained to lead Christ's priestly people (of whom they are a part) in Christian life and worship. The close relationship among these three meanings is very important to maintain, for out of it comes a viable understanding of priests today and how they are being called to serve the Church and lead it into the fullest expression of its role as the sacrament of God.

The teaching and reforms of the Second Vatican Council, especially in the area of worship and sacraments, were the fruit of a century of scholarship and pastoral developments. Reflecting on these theological developments, the council chose to describe the Church itself as a sacrament, desiring that all the baptized should become light for the world and a transforming grace in society. In this sense, Christians—all Christians—live a sacramental existence that manifests their connection with Christ through the power of the Holy Spirit. They are visible expressions of Christ who is the primordial sacrament of humanity's encounter with God.

"Since the church, in Christ, is a sacrament—a sign and instrument, that is, of communion with God and of the unity of the entire human race—it here proposes, for the benefit of the faithful and of the entire world, to describe more clearly . . . its own nature and universal mission." (*LG* §1)

21

THE PRIESTHOOD OF CHRIST

"Since, then, we have a great high priest who has passed through the heavens, Jesus, the Son of God, let us hold fast to our confession. For we do not have a high priest who is unable to sympathize with our weaknesses, but we have one who in every respect has been tested as we are, yet without sin. Let us therefore approach the throne of grace with boldness, so that we may receive mercy and find grace to help in time of need."
(Heb 4:14-16)

Christ is the source of all Christian life. Sent from God, begotten both of God and of a human mother, Christ is brother and friend of those who receive him and the bridge between God and ourselves. He is our mediator, priest, sacrifice, and reconciliation. Although he was born into the Hebrew religious tradition of Temple priesthood that repeated prescribed acts of sacrifice in hopes of effecting atonement for sin and offering thanksgiving for the goods of life, the Palestinian Jew Jesus Christ brought about a new age. As Hebrews puts it succinctly, "by a single offering he has perfected for all time those who are sanctified" (Heb 10:14).

Through the Temple sacrifices, those living on earth cried out to God beyond their reach, for mercy. But this ancient structure of sacrifices repeated again and again was supplanted by the incarnation of God's own son. God thus linked heaven and earth, the divine and the human, to reconcile us sinful creatures and to offer grace, friendship, and holiness to those who receive his son.

In the Letter to the Hebrews Christ is called the perfect high priest. Although Son of God, he took our human frailty, weaknesses, and mortality upon himself. He is the fulfillment of the Old Covenant symbolized by the priesthood of Aaron, but he inaugurated the New Covenant symbolized by the priesthood of Melchizedek. The sacrifices of Aaron and the Levites—grain offerings, bulls, goats, doves, or blood poured out—were repeated every year according to the season and the feast. But the sacrifice of Christ is not the offering of something other than himself; rather, it is the immolation of his very life. It is a victory over death and the remedy for sin.

The sacrifices of the Old Covenant were offered in an earthly sanctuary, the Jerusalem Temple built by human hands. But Christ passed through death into a sanctuary not made by human hands. His perfect offering, which is both human and divine, is not being lifted up to God in anxious entreaty. Rather he presents it in the very presence of his Father and so achieves what the sacrifices of the Old Covenant could never do. For Christ breaks through the veil that separates mortal from immortal, earthly from heavenly, and time from eternity. This is how Christ becomes "the mediator of a new covenant" (Heb 9:15) and how "he has appeared once for all . . . to remove sin by the sacrifice of himself" (Heb 9:26).

The author of Hebrews notes that, "if he were on earth . . . [Christ] would not be a priest at all, since there are priests who offer gifts according to the law"(8:4). Even in heaven, his sacrifice of immolation behind him, he does not stand over an altar renewing his sacrifice for sins; rather "when Christ had offered for all time a single sacrifice for sins, 'he sat down at the right hand of God.' . . . For by a single offering, he has perfected for all time those who are sanctified" (10:12-14).

THE PRIESTHOOD OF THE FAITHFUL

What Christ now offers to the Father in his eternal priestly act is what he has won by the mystery of his redemptive incarnation. He hands over to the Father the body that he assumed in both its aspects—his "resurrection body" that is the fruit of his triumph over death and his "mystical body" that includes all the members joined to him by baptism in the Holy Spirit. The baptized faithful share in his "priestly office of offering spiritual worship for the glory of the Father and the salvation of humanity" (*LG* §34).

The priestly actions of the baptized are united to Christ's heavenly priesthood. As Vatican II teaches: "their prayers and apostolic undertakings, family and married life, daily work, relaxation of mind and body, even the hardships of life if patiently borne . . . are offered to the Father in all piety along with the body of the Lord. And so, worshiping everywhere by their holy actions, the laity consecrate the world itself to God" (*LG* §34).

In virtue of their baptism, all the faithful participate in the priesthood of Christ. The *Catechism of the Catholic Church* expresses this as follows: "The ministerial or hierarchical priesthood of bishops and priests, and the common priesthood of all the faithful participate, each in its own proper way in the one priesthood of Christ" (§1547). In the same place the *Catechism* cites this text of St. Thomas Aquinas: "Only Christ is the true priest, the others being only his ministers" (§1545).

The priesthood of the faithful gets the most attention in the New Testament. First Peter 2:9 explains that the faithful are "a chosen race, a royal priesthood, a holy nation" and "God's own people" who have been called to make manifest God's continuing action in the world. In offering sanctified lives to God "along with the Body of

"I remember the president of the Lutheran Church in America telling me, 'I get many questions from Roman Catholics, and a very common one is, "Who is the head of your church?" My answer to them is, "The head of my church is the same as the head of your church, Jesus Christ."' He is right, but unfortunately we would not always recognize that." (Brown 1980, 13)

the Lord" (*LG* §34), the faithful express the triumph of enduring faith over the materialism and cynicism that surround them. They enter the mystery of Christ's "Passover," learning to persevere through obstacles and hardships in uniting their lives, their work, and their relationships to Christ's gift of himself to his Father.

They live with hope through painful marriages, troubled parenting, unwelcome integrity at work, or wounded friendships, finding in Christ the "pioneer and perfecter of our faith" (Heb 12:2). Their loving acts of ministry, generosity, justice, and compassion are the visible expression of the living Christ, animating his mystical body. This priestly life of the baptized expresses the dynamic nature of the Church as the sacrament of God. It is the means for God's actual transformation of the world.

THE MINISTERIAL PRIESTHOOD

Again the *Catechism* clarifies this: "While the common priesthood of the faithful is exercised by the unfolding of baptismal grace—a life of faith, hope, and charity, a life according to the Spirit—the ministerial priesthood is at the service of the common priesthood. It is directed at the unfolding of the baptismal grace of all Christians" (§1547). The ordained have as their mission to gather, proclaim, explain, heal, nourish, and send the people whom God has chosen through baptism to be his own. The ordained foster the social and theological reality of a priestly people by living closely with them and teaching them the dynamics of Christ's paschal mystery in their lives. Vatican II left no doubt about its fundamental vision of the Church's mission:

"The apostolate of the laity is a sharing in the Church's saving mission. . . . The laity . . . are given this special vocation: to make the Church present and fruitful in those places and circumstances where it is only through them that it can become the salt of the earth" (*LG* §33). The Church, after being gathered around the table of the Eucharist, is then scattered to generate fruitful life as a transforming presence in the world. The deepest joy of the bishop and of his assisting priests is to oversee the apostolic action of the faithful. The *Catechism* explains: "Through the ordained ministry, especially that of bishops and priests, the presence of Christ as head of

"In New Testament times, there seems to have been a special stress on offering one's life as a sacrifice for those who had not yet heard of Christ, so that they could see in Christian dedication a challenge to believe. 1 Peter 2:12 goes on to say that Christians are so to live among the Gentiles that they will see their good deeds and glorify God." (Brown 1980, 14)

"[Following the recitation of the narrative of the Lord's institution of the sacrament of his body and blood, the bishop or priest then] prays to the Father to send his Spirit and make everybody into 'one body, one Spirit in Christ.' After the resurrection and Pentecost, Christ exists only as the total Christ." (*The Holy Spirit, Lord and Giver of Life* 112–13)

the church is made visible in the midst of the community of believers" (§1549).

The ministerial priesthood is a service to the people of God. Priests, entrusted with a divine ministry by their bishops, are ordained to fulfill the work of Christ on behalf of his members. This consists in preaching the Gospel (*LG* §28 and *PO* §4), shepherding the faithful, and celebrating divine worship. Acting on behalf of Christ, priests proclaim his mystery, unite the prayers and sacrifices of the faithful to Christ their head, and in the Mass renew the unique sacrifice of the New Testament, making it present to the Church gathered.

Under the authority of their bishops, priests minister to the people assigned to them, making the universal Church visible within their particular situation. They become spiritual fathers in Christ for the faithful whom they beget by baptism and holy teaching (*LG* §28). This relationship is expressed in their compassionate availability to believers and unbelievers alike. Their responsibility for their people, like that of parents for their family, must be discharged with integrity and authority. Their real effectiveness will depend upon good relationships of mutual trust and genuine love.

This theological vision of presbyteral ministry can be summarized in terms of some very definite theological priorities. Presbyteral ministry must be defined in broad pastoral—not uniquely liturgical—terms. We need to reshape our imagination of priestly ministry, shifting it from cultic to comprehensive. The central importance of preaching, called by Vatican II the primary responsibility of the ordained, is based on the fact that the word of God is the very source of the Church's life. Ongoing catechesis is the foundation (often a missing foundation) for the effective Christian life of the faithful.

"The people of God is formed into one in the first place by the word of the living God, which is quite rightly expected from the mouth of priests. For since nobody can be saved who has not first believed, it is the first task of priests as co-workers of the bishops to preach the Gospel of God to all." *PO* §4

The Synergy of the Two Earthly Priesthoods

Ordained ministry is rooted in Christ's unique priesthood. All the baptized, ordained and nonordained, are a priestly people because through their baptism they offer "spiritual sacrifices" to the Father along with the body of the Lord. Further, in a unique way, bishops and presbyters express Christ's priesthood by acting in the name of the body of Christ *(corpus ecclesiae)* and of the person of Christ *(in persona Christi)* in calling together, presiding over, and ministering to the people of God. Bishops and presbyters are members of that body themselves, as equally graced as the laity by the mercy of divine adoption, although their special ministry is to offer sacramental headship in the body's worship, ministry, and common life.

It is wrong to separate the common priesthood by which the baptized offer spiritual sacrifices to God from the ministerial priesthood. Likewise, it is wrong to imagine the apostolic ministry of the ordained apart from the apostolic fruitfulness of the baptized. From the moment of our baptism, our lives are joined to Christ and our lives become a priestly offering to God. (The First Letter of Peter, which names the faithful as a "priestly people" [cf. 2:9], is in all likelihood a baptismal catechesis from the first century.) Yet we have been cautioned so urgently to remember that the priesthood of the faithful and the ministerial priesthood "differ essentially and not only in degree" (*LG* §10) that we have tended to lose the missionary focus of the Church and deprive the faithful of any awareness of their priestly identity.

Is the more urgent pastoral problem before the Church today that the ordained will lose sight of this "essential" distinction? Or is it not rather that most Catholics have no idea of the priesthood of all believers and are not able to understand or accept it? The latter situation encourages the sad possibility that people will live their participation in the sufferings of Christ without any understanding of its sacramental meaning or its apostolic fruitfulness.

In any case, it makes no sense to talk about ministerial priesthood without talking simultaneously about the spiritual sacrifices that Christians offer, even as they receive the gift of God communicated to them in the Eucharist. The Eucharist is for the sake of building up the body of Christ, which is the end and goal of all ministry. As Paul writes, "The gifts he gave were that some would be apostles, some prophets, some evangelists, some pastors and teachers, to equip the saints for the work of ministry, for building up the body of Christ" (Eph 4:11).

For all the faithful who have become "one body, one Spirit in Christ" through a common sacramental life, the presbyter offers apostolic leadership, pastoral friendship, unifying solidarity, education in the life of prayer, and the example of a life given over to the gospel in his kingly role as pastor (cf. *PO* §6).

> "Theoretically, we have always acknowledged this general priesthood; but as I remember hearing of it in theology studies, it was always with a caution: 'Remember that there is a metaphysical difference between the ordained priesthood and the priesthood of the faithful, a difference of kind, not just of degree.' But does not our emphasis have to be in the other direction, not cautionary but encouraging?"
> (Brown 1980, 15)

> "Through the ministry of priests, the spiritual sacrifice of the faithful is completed in union with the sacrifice of Christ the only mediator, which in the Eucharist is offered through the priest's hands in the name of the whole church in an unbloody and sacramental manner until the Lord himself shall come."
> (*PO* §1)

THE CHALLENGES OF LAY MINISTRY

The most successful example of the intentional appropriation by the faithful of their apostolic calling in the years since Vatican II has been the growth of lay ecclesial ministry in the American Church. For thirty years, the core personnel for the Church's catechetical ministry have been lay faithful. Today there are more professional ecclesial lay ministers working in American parishes than there are ordained priests. This great gift of lay apostolic service has become the frame for several important questions for the future of Catholic pastoral life.

Pope John Paul II has warned against the clericalization of lay elites (*CL* §23). It is evident that the diminishing numbers of ordained presbyters and the growing expectations for developing ministries make the employment of the laity in auxiliary pastoral roles both reasonable and necessary. However, Pope John Paul II has articulated his disappointment that the talent and enthusiasm of the most gifted lay faithful are first drawn into liturgical ministries. He fears that this may be to the detriment of lay witness and committed political action as Christians in the world.

This hoped-for lay apostolic presence in the world, which was one of the major themes of the Council documents of the 1960s, has seldom received the theological development, catechesis, or implementation consistent with its importance as a major theme of the Council. The texts of *Lumen Gentium* (The Constitution on the Church) about the laity's role in bringing the Church's mission to the world that we cited above are rarely part of the common store of Sunday preaching.

On the positive side, one of the real benefits of having laity serve in ministerial functions is the real and symbolic solidarity which they express with the other laity of the parish. While half of those professionally engaged in Catholic lay ecclesial ministry possess a master's degree (or higher) in pastoral studies, many of those in such roles do not possess adequate pastoral or theological formation. A healthy ecclesiology focused upon lay apostolic presence in the world ought to be an essential prerequisite for pastoral leadership (for both ordained and non-ordained ministers). Without such a missionary ecclesiology, it is possible to imagine that the Church exists essentially in order to celebrate its liturgical rites, and one could lose sight of the Church's mission as bearer of the Good News about the kingdom of God.

"The primary and immediate task [of lay people] is not to establish and develop the ecclesial community—this is the specific role of the pastors—but to put to use every Christian and evangelical possibility latent but already present and active in the affairs of the world." (*EN* §70)

"When we look at the total picture of parish ministers, religious and lay, part-timers and full-timers, four out of five have a college education and 53.5 percent have at least a master's degree—a well-educated cadre of parish ministers." (Murnion and DeLambo 1999, 29)

The lack of a missionary ecclesiology in many parishes may be linked to the general failure of adult catechesis in the postconciliar years. The absence of clear structures for adult faith formation in so many Catholic parishes is a major concern of the American bishops for the future (see *Our Hearts Were Burning within Us,* USCCB). The U.S. Church has one of the highest attendance rates for Sunday Mass in the world (27% weekly, 50% monthly). France's attendance rate is only around 23% weekly, Spain's is about the same. Yet we must ask, as the bishops' pastoral statement does ask: Do our people understand the mystery that they celebrate? Do they know how to live the mystery of the Christian life? Do they understand the dignity and the power of their baptismal priesthood?

The paschal mystery of Christ is the heart of all Christian spirituality. It is by understanding our participation in the priesthood of Christ, who offers to the Father the spiritual sacrifices that we live out in our own lives, that we see how the paschal mystery becomes fruitful for ourselves and for others. The Church interprets the theological identity of the ministerial priest in terms of his spiritual and pastoral leadership of a priestly people. "In the service of the common priesthood," as the *Catechism* puts it, the ordained ministry of the Catholic priest is expressed in a comprehensive repertory of roles that assure the spiritual health and growth in faith of God's people gathered as Church.

How is this leadership concretely expressed today in the midst of so many changes in Church and society? Chapter 4 will give a picture of the comprehensive dynamics of the ministry of the ordained in the context of today's Church.

Agenda for Personal and Group Reflections

QUESTIONS FOR THE INDIVIDUAL PRIEST

1. How seriously have I taken the teaching that the Church is a sacrament of Christ and its people the visible sign?

2. How would I go about preaching the Catholic teaching about the priesthood of the faithful? In what ways would this be important for my people?

3. How is my calling "to be at the service of the common priesthood" concretely going to shape my ministry?

4. Have I provided my lay associates and assistants who aid me in the pastoral work of the parish opportunities to study and discuss with me their role in the ministry? Do they have a vision of an apostolic laity? What difference does it make if they do?

5. What other questions have emerged for me from reflecting on the Church's doctrine about the three priesthoods?

QUESTIONS FOR GROUP DISCUSSION

1. How do we understand the joining of the "spiritual sacrifices" of the common priesthood to the one eternal sacrifice of Christ?

2. What does it mean theologically to say with Aquinas that Christ is the only true priest? How does that help us understand our own ministerial priesthood?

3. Do we need a diocesan-wide catechesis on priesthood that will awaken the faithful to their priestly character? If we did this, what would the essential points be?

4. What effort have we made in our diocese and in our parishes to enable our laity to comprehend their own irreplaceable role in evangelization? How would taking the perspective of a "mission ecclesiology" change the way we preach or celebrate?

5. If you could have been personally present for one of the Lord's mysteries during his lifetime, which one would you choose? Why that particular one?

6. What are the strengths and weaknesses that priests bring to their service of the common priesthood? How can they be helped to maximize their strengths and minimize their weaknesses?

Chapter Four

The Shape of Ordained Ministry Today

Priests today have to negotiate a complicated world of people who expect vastly different things of them. Super-conservative Catholics want them to be enforcers of Church law (as they construe it) and exacting celebrants of liturgies precisely as they are written in the official books (and nothing more). Others expect signs of openness toward diversity, among other things inclusive language and representative modeling of cultural diversity in the choice of readers, acolytes, musicians, extraordinary ministers of the Eucharist, and the like. Some parishioners think of the Mass as a form of divine theater that they want to be awe-inspiring and distant. Others recognize parish liturgies as the people's celebration in the here and now within which the eucharistic memorial is celebrated. Priests can be torn apart, or at least shaken up, by these contradictory demands. Their sharing in the paschal mystery of Jesus is often linked concretely to tensions of this very kind. What are they really expected to do?

Because of the waves of change that have washed over both Church and society since Vatican II, most Catholics recognize that the ministerial priesthood has been transformed in significant ways. We have already reviewed a number of ways in which these changes may be described. We also looked at Christian priesthood in New Testament terms and observed the immense importance of ordained ministry in providing strong, sympathetic, and faithful leadership for those living the common priesthood of the baptized.

We mentioned before that an exclusively cultic understanding of ordained or ministerial priesthood is inadequate. Rather, Catholic ministerial priesthood should be understood in a comprehensive way. So in this chapter, we explore the nature of ordained ministry in the Catholic Church by examining six roles that have emerged more clearly in the forty years since the convoking of the Second Vatican Council. They are integral parts of a fully functioning and spiritually vital priestly life. These descriptions are derived from the Council documents, from pastoral reflection and writing in recent decades, and, above all, from the actual experience of presbyteral ministry.

Six Roles Exercised by the Ordained

The multiple roles of the ordained are spelled out here in terms of six categories: (1) vicar of the bishop, (2) bearer of the mystery, (3) spiritual personality, (4) pastoral leader, (5) model of human authenticity, and (6) prophet. There may be some overlap between these categories. We hope that by spelling out some of the obvious meanings of each of the categories, we will help bishops and priests recognize their own ministry and spirituality in what we describe. Further, by identifying these distinct dimensions of priestly ministry, we hope to help readers understand and appropriate the ideas and values that we have named.

(1) The vicar of the bishop. In the prayer of ordination of a presbyter (1990), the bishop prays, "And now we ask you, Lord: in our weakness give us also the helpers that we need to exercise the priesthood that comes from the apostles." That same understanding of the presbyter as the helper and support of the bishop is expressed in *Lumen Gentium* (§28): "Presbyters, prudent cooperators of the episcopal college and its support and instrument, called to the service of the people of God, constitute, together with their bishop, one presbyterate, though dedicated to a variety of duties. In each local assembly of the faithful they make the bishop present, in a sense, and they are associated with him in trust and generosity; for their part they take upon themselves his duties and solicitude and carry them out in their daily work for the faithful."

So priests are official representatives of the bishop who speak with authority and are empowered by the Church through the bishop. They interpret the Church's tradition of faith and practice and sanctify and govern the people assigned to them. They convene and preside over the assemblies of the faithful. They are the visible sign of unity in the parish community, and through their loyalty to their bishop, they exercise a ministry of unity in the diocese. The council goes on to say: "Presbyters for their part should keep in mind the fullness of the sacrament of order which bishops enjoy and should reverence in their persons the authority of Christ the supreme Pastor" (*PO* §7). The sacred powers of priests extend the ministry of the bishop in scope and variety.

Their common relationship to the bishop in obedience and filial affection, loyalty and willing cooperation, should establish a bond of unity among priests. The council describes them as "an intimate sacramental brotherhood" (*PO* §8). Their readiness to help one another, whether diocesan or regular, flows from the very nature of the presbyteral order. The brotherly bond that exists among them means that they have an obligation to care for one another and a responsibility toward those in difficulty. It also means taking time to help one another, "even discreetly warning them when necessary"(ibid.).

Older priests should recognize their responsibility to mentor, teach, support, and encourage those new to ministry or struggling, for some reason or other, to make sense of their call. "They should be particularly concerned about those who are sick, about the afflicted, the overworked, the lonely, the exiled, [and] the persecuted. They should also be happy to gather together for relaxation" in order to share mutual support and friendship (*PO* §8).

The role of priests as the bishop's vicar implies both courage and humility. They courageously represent the Church's authority and compassion as the voice of the bishop who is the chief representative of Christ in the local Church. For his part, the bishop is encouraged to know his priests deeply and well, to listen carefully to their analysis of the needs and possibilities of the diocesan church, and to be accessible and genuine with them—truly a father figure. This implies humility on the part of priests and deference in their obedience to the pastoral judgment and ecclesial discipline of the bishop as the leader of the local church. These days, initiatives are appropriate and required in both directions between bishops and priests, if real fraternal solidarity in the one priesthood they share is to be authentic.

"In all forms of liturgical prayer, but preeminently in the Holy Eucharist, [the priest] is ritualizing the interaction in his ministry. Standing in the place of the bishop (and thus ritualizing that ministerial relationship), he leads his community into an experience of the communion of the Church by mediating and exemplifying reconciliation." (*SR* 23)

The Shape of Ordained Ministry Today   33

Religious priests, whose ordinary is not the local bishop but their own major superior, form a special category in this regard. The charism of their founder and the mission of their religious institute constitute a pastoral value that is placed at the service of the local ordinary and the diocese. For his part, the bishop should carefully consider the charism of religious institutes and their potential to serve the spiritual needs of the diocese (*VC* §48–50). Religious, for their part, owe the bishop respect, affection, and obedience in the decisions that govern their participation in the ministry of the local church.

The spirituality of both bishops and priests will be nurtured by the development of mutual trust and common concerns. At the very least, both bishop and priests need to remember and reverence the fact that it is God who has called them to their offices of pastoral service. With God's grace, the council's words will prove to be a living reality: "On account of [their] common sharing in the same priesthood and ministry, bishops are to regard their priests as brothers and friends and are to take the greatest possible interest in their welfare both temporal and spiritual." And priests "should . . . be attached to their bishop with sincere charity and obedience" (*PO* §7).

"I use the term [presbyter] as [the] expression of the fact that the ordained priest is part of a body of ministers sharing the responsibility of the bishop. It is the relationship of priests with one another and with the bishop that is at stake here. Both relationships are being renegotiated. . . . [O]nly a quarter of the priests in the Hoge study find strong support for their priestly ministry from their bishop."
(Murnion 2002, 10)

The relationship just described is a serious challenge for many priests, since it does not fit their experienced reality. Some priests wonder if they can trust their bishop to be their advocate and friend after the bishops' *Charter for the Protection of Children and Young People* made so many concessions injurious to due process for priests. It is time for us to be called back to what the gospel expects of us and to the ideal that the Vatican II documents eloquently describe. Honest dialogue about their relationship is clearly warranted.

(2) Bearer of the Mystery (Mystagogue). The presbyter is the teacher of the Church's holy mysteries. As the Council puts it: "The people of God is formed into one in the first place by the word of the living God, which is quite rightly expected from the mouth of presbyters"(*PO* §4). The term mystagogue, or bearer of the mystery, means someone who teaches the divine mysteries. Long neglected in the Western Church, the term came back into use along with the widespread implementation of the Rite of Christian Initiation of Adults. The catechumenal process was designed to lead adult candidates for baptism into full communion with the Church. Consequent upon

their reception of the sacrament of baptism, the newly initiated enter a period of instruction still known by the Greek term, mystagogy.

As practiced by the great Fathers of the fourth century, especially St. Cyril of Jerusalem, mystagogy was an explanation and interpretation of the rites of the Church's liturgy in terms of their meaning for the faith and fellowship of the baptized. More simply, mystagogy presupposes the need for an ongoing catechesis for adult Christians, rooted in community and liturgy.

The need for this has been highlighted by the pastoral plan for adult faith formation, *Our Hearts Were Burning Within Us,* published by the U.S. bishops in 1999. As that document says rather starkly: "Many Catholics seem 'lukewarm' in faith or have a limited understanding of what the Church believes, is, and lives. . . . For a variety of reasons, people leave the Church. They may seek out or be recruited into non-denominational, evangelical, or fundamentalist churches, or into New Age or other religious movements. Far too often they simply abandon the Christian faith altogether"(§§35–36). Adult faith formation *is* mystagogy. It has as its goal to lead people to become committed disciples of Jesus Christ. Its aim is to create an apostolic laity who possess a faith that is "living, explicit, and fruitful," to use the expression of the bishops' document.

Mystagogy seeks to enable a genuine and deep conversion to Jesus in holiness of life. It aims to move Christian faith from the *notional* to the *real,* to use an expression of Cardinal Newman. Christian faith is not about "ideas one has thought," but about "a divine relationship fully lived." We need to lead our people to understand the holy signs that we celebrate. It is our job to allow the rites to speak as fully as they can through the quality of our performance of the liturgy. As bearers of the mystery, our ritual leadership will invest the sacraments with dignity and integrity. This helps the faithful see how the rites express God's presence, God's claim upon them, and their vocation to become living witnesses to the Church as a sign and sacrament of salvation.

The missionary ecclesiology of a priestly people can only emerge from lay faithful who are living a transforming faith. The pressure of numbers and the limited cadre of priests often make us settle for sacramental celebrations that are religious but not really faith experiences. They are religious because they address the craving of

"Laity look to sermons that speak of God experientially; they reject liturgies that do not breathe the presence of God. . . . People across the country search out the priest who seems to be able to put them in touch with God, to mediate God to themselves and in this fashion to be the 'sign and agent of reconciliation.'" (*SR* 11–12)

those who come for spiritual comfort and some level of religious nurture. But they are not faith experiences in the full sense because the people do not understand the fundamental realities that the liturgy celebrates: that the sacraments are the common work of a priestly people, that what we offer to God is the sacrifice of the whole Christ—the Head and members together, and that the "Church gathered" has been called together to be sent out on mission to proclaim the kingdom of God.

In terms of priestly spirituality, being a bearer of the mystery demands an appreciation of ritual, a symbolic literacy, and a passion to share the meaning of the liturgy. The mystagogue can never be satisfied to allow the holy signs that the Church celebrates to become merely a means of satisfying human curiosity or a craving for religious experience. Rather he will work unceasingly to explain the unspeakable mercy of adoption, whereby God adds men and women to the body of Christ through the sacraments and the gifts of the Holy Spirit.

The part of priesthood most priests like best—sacramental celebration, especially the Mass—is the work of the bearer of the mystery. Presiding at Eucharist with transparent faith and commitment is a powerful sign of the priest's depth of surrender to the mysteries of Christ in his own life and an invitation to people to enter along with him into the mysteries. A good mystagogue will be impatient to have his people understand and love the full meaning of the rites they celebrate.

Priests proclaim and explain God's revelation through preaching and catechesis. They are committed to adult faith formation and to forming baptized apostles to assist him in the work of evangelization. This is not so hard to do, but we have long neglected it. As our bishops recently acknowledged, without this missing link, the mystery of salvation is unable to express itself and to transform the world. While there are many obstacles to adult catechesis, experience shows that it can be done. The bishops say in their conclusion, "Jesus the Risen One is still with us, meeting us on the pathways of our lives, sharing our concerns, enlightening us with his word, strengthening us with his presence, nourishing us in the breaking of the bread, and sending us forth to be his witnesses" (OHB §182).

Finally, the task of evangelization is the work of the bearer of the mystery. As Cardinal Avery Dulles, citing Cardinal Joseph Ratzinger, summarizes this role: "The priest is not primarily a cultic figure but an evangelist.

"People are hungry for God. Look at the books on angels and after-death themes. The bookstore shelves are full of them, as well as writings on scripture and the spiritual life. And people are buying. Priests are here to point people toward the authentic gospel, to celebrate with them the key sacramental themes in their lives that are so meaningful even to indifferent Catholics." (William J. Bausch in Friedl and Reynolds 1997, 106)

"Especially as he celebrates the Mass, [the priest] personifies the convergence of death and resurrection as he proclaims the mystery of faith: Christ has died, Christ is risen, Christ will come again." (SR 23)

"How does the sacramental ministry of the priest contribute to his own holiness? As minister he makes present in visible, tangible form the death and resurrection of Christ, the proof and sign of God's love. . . . He thus in a special way is the mediator of reconciliation, liberation, new life in Christ." (SR 22)

The priority of the word, however, does not displace the sacramental or pastoral dimensions. Word and sacrament are inseparable" (Dulles 1997, 22). In Pope Paul VI's vision of evangelization, "Evangelizing . . . is the grace and vocation proper to the church, its deepest identity. It exists in order to evangelize, which means in the first place to preach and to teach" (Dulles 1997, 23). Priests have to develop a living hunger to draw both the baptized and those outside the Church into a fruitful knowledge of and obedience to God's word. Evangelizing activities may be shared by others, but the stewardship of this ministry belongs by right to priests in cooperation with their bishops. They constantly seek to open the doors of the Church to those who seek for God and want to know God's will.

"In order to perform this service [of preaching the word of God], the priest must have intimate personal knowledge of the word of God. He should know the scripture not only in its exegetical and linguistic aspects, but also in such a way that he puts on the mind of Christ, letting the word of God penetrate his thoughts and feelings." (Dulles 1997, 25)

(3) Spiritual personality. Priestly ministry requires a healthy inner life. American media culture, at its worst, seems to be totally dedicated to the promotion of the un-reflective life—to the impossibility of an inner life. There is no public place where one can go without being bombarded by talk, noise, advertising, and incessant interruptions. Yet, hard as it may be, it is important for priests to claim an inner life for themselves through keeping a journal, practicing contemplative prayer, writing poetry, making retreats, or reading and taking time for the spiritual life. Otherwise they, like most adults in our society, will find themselves overwhelmed by the intrusive demands of our consumer culture.

Many priests and seminarians have been wounded emotionally or even physically or psychically abused in their younger lives. Children of divorce, of alcoholic parents, of households where both parents worked full time, they had to be resourceful enough to create a world for themselves. Unfortunately what was modeled for many of them was the incessant use of television as a distraction and as a narcotic. As adults, we have to renegotiate our terms with the culture in which we live.

Finding a true inner life requires nothing less than heroism for many seminarians and priests. Yet the role they have been called to fulfill requires modeling intimacy with God. To achieve growth in communion with God requires the best of their strength and their heartiest determination. People expect this quality of spiritual depth of a priest.

Today, for many people, one of the most obvious avenues of entry into the Church is through the Church's

"Because the clatter of radio and television inundate one's life with the preoccupations of the whole world and in the process often drown out the peace and self-possession needed for a life of faith, a person may have to withdraw periodically from these channels of communication. Only persons who possess their souls, who are willing to take time to reflect on their own experience, to tune into themselves, in a word, simply 'to be' are suitable subjects for [a prayer of dialogue with God]." (*SR* 31)

spiritual tradition. In addition to the appeal of Catholic liturgy for many outside the Church, there is also the immense treasure of the Church's mystical tradition: her spiritual writers, her art treasures, her sacred music, and her tradition of contemplation. As leaders of Christian communities, priests are gatekeepers to these spiritual treasures through the programs they create, the preaching they do, and the witness of their own lives.

Not everyone who is ordained will have broad or deep culture. However, all priests can be expected to manifest a mature discipline in faith and religious practice as a public witness for the community. Time for spiritual reading, time for a prayer that is essentially "listening to God," time for periods of spiritual rest—these are practices that shape a person profoundly. By familiarity with the things of God, priests draw to themselves those who are seeking a close relationship with the divine.

The Council sets a very high standard for priests as ministers of holiness. Like all the baptized, priests are called to the perfection of holiness (*LG* §40). But by ordination, they are consecrated to God in a new way to be instruments of the holiness of Christ. "By the grace [of his priesthood] the priest, through his service of the people committed to his care and all the people of God, is able the better to pursue the perfection of Christ, whose place he takes. The human weakness of his flesh is remedied by the holiness of him who became for us a high priest" (*PO* §12; cf. Heb 7:26). The idea is clear: the presbyter is called to be a minister of holiness by example and by spiritual guidance for the people given to his care. What the council document does not stress as much are these two points: how urgent this ministry of holiness is, and how difficult are the demands that it makes upon the individual who is ordained.

Many priests will benefit from working with a regular spiritual director. We will mention this idea again elsewhere, but it pertains to this role of spiritual personality. Spiritual direction is a time of accountability, healing, encouragement, enlightening interpretation, and the sacramental ministration of the Holy Spirit's guidance and love. It cannot be recommended too highly.

For many priests, support groups and regular faith sharing with other priests (and laity as well) provide the counterpart to the ministry of individual spiritual direction. However one finally goes about it, it will be the case that a healthy spiritual personality does not try to live the Christian spiritual life in isolation.

"If the priest is to be a mediator between heaven and earth, if he is to speak symbolically of the all-embracing and ever elusive mystery of Being itself, he must be in habitual contact with the Mystery, he must stand stubbornly in the presence of God." (Barron 1996, 96)

(4) *Pastoral leader.* Pastors have the responsibility to promote cooperation among their people, to call forth their gifts, to welcome their imagination and creativity, and to generate among them an expectation for rich collaboration among all the serious Christians in the parish. We mentioned two realities that have transformed parish life: the multiplication of ministries (and the concomitant responsibility to form and oversee them) and the great diversity among people distinct in their generational outlook, their cultural background, and their ideological concerns. Figuring out how to allocate time and resources in the midst of such diversity can be excruciating.

Many priests find the responsibilities of physical maintenance of the parish plant; monitoring the budget; hiring and supervising; evaluating and directing personnel; and submitting reports, collections, and planning documents to diocesan officials very difficult. Most priests were never trained to read budgets, to plan a capital campaign, to evaluate personnel, or to do many other things that risk taking up the majority of their time. When half of pastoral leadership equates with plant administration, it's time for a radical reevaluation of the ministry.

Other people can prepare budgets, chair development meetings, write draft reports, and do similar things. No one else but the pastor is able to set the tone for real collaboration in the ministries of parish worship, education, social service, and community building. In most large parishes today, there are five to ten religious and lay people associated with parish education, liturgy, and the administration of the other works of the parish. Ensuring good communication with his coworkers, dreaming out loud with them about the needs of the parish, and making sure to have regular staff meetings that include genuine common prayer—these are the priorities among priorities. This kind of leadership requires selfless dedication, courage, competence, and decisiveness, no matter what style of personality the priest may possess.

Most priests and seminarians entered the seminary because they dreamed of helping other people grow in the faith and know God more deeply. Most never realized how complicated the structure of a parish community can be. Unprepared for the work of administration, many priests bluff their way for years through the bureaucratic details of finance and administration. But the buck stops on the pastor's desk. Still, something can be done to help priests

"Priests today locate their relationship with Christ in real life, as did the disciples on the road to Emmaus, because this is the place of encounter with him. . . . There is, first of all, a human sharing between the two disconsolate disciples and the stranger. This dialogue becomes the human foundation for an explicit sharing of faith." (*SR* 32)

"Some priests are better administrators, counselors, teachers, or confessors. Priests themselves need to recognize and accept these differences. Others can assist them by encouraging their talents while also accepting their limitations." (Quartier 1999, 80)

> "An effective evaluation tool to help presbyters recognize their talents and weak points would be of great help in matching individual priests with the needs of a particular parish. This might prevent many frustrations and dashed expectations from both priest and parish." (Quartier 1999, 80)

> "He is only a minister. It is Jesus who saves. The death of the Lord Jesus has given free access to the Father to all who believe (Rom 5:2); the kingdom of God is among us and the Church is the privileged depository and vehicle of salvation. The priest is only steward and dispenser of the mysteries of God." (*SR* 12)

lighten the load of their bureaucracy. There are workshops for learning about pastoral administration. There are ways of building a parish pastoral council. And there are ways of creating a staff that is genuinely collaborative.

The bottom line is this: even as a pastoral leader/ administrator, the priest is a symbol of Christ's pastoral grace. Some of the concerns here are considerations of justice. Clear role expectations, agreed upon compensation for full-time ministry offered by lay ecclesial ministers, regular staff meetings professionally executed, and opportunities for consultation and initiatives from the laity of the parish are all areas that require a pastor's respect and attention. In all of these cases, there is a learning curve: many of the skills needed to be a good pastoral leader come from practice.

With respect to spirituality, the most important issue here is the priest's humility to acknowledge his inabilities or limitations and to seek the training and the resources needed to create a serene and effective life. The asceticism of parish leadership for many pastors is the sheer attrition of difficult jobs for which they are not properly trained. But there's plenty of pastoral asceticism to go around without taking on the drain of unnecessary pain and anxiety.

Modeling responsibility and collaboration, with a priority upon spiritual leadership, is one of the strongest contributions a priest can make as a pastoral leader. His leadership implies the habit of making other people successful. He is responsible to see that the parish's leaders have and share a gospel vision. He is the pastor of his coworkers as well as of the parish faithful. His mandate is not just to administer the status quo, but to grow in understanding and passion for a shared Christian life that will make a difference in his own life and the lives of his community. When that dimension of his pastoral leadership is foremost, he is usually a contented man.

(5) A model of human authenticity. In his apostolic exhortation, *Pastores Dabo Vobis* (*I Will Give You Shepherds,* 1992), Pope John Paul II explains how "human formation [is] the basis of all priestly formation" (*PDV* §43). His fundamental theme here is that the priest "should seek to reflect in himself . . . the human perfection which shines forth in the Incarnate Son of God and which is reflected with particular liveliness in his attitudes toward others as we see narrated in the Gospels." The Pope argues that for

the ministry of the priest to be humanly credible and as attractive as possible, the ordained should shape his personality so that "it becomes a bridge and not an obstacle for others in their meeting with Jesus Christ."

The Pope's concerns are many. Priests should be able to read hearts, that is, perceive people's difficulties and problems, and extend themselves to make conversation and dialogue easily and pleasantly. They need to have the depth of maturity that will create trust in others and invite their cooperation. They should be known as persons who remain serene under pressure and can be objective in making difficult judgments. So priests need to cultivate a range of human qualities not only for the sake of their own maturity, but also with a view to the ministry. As the Pope says again:

These qualities are needed for them to be balanced people, strong and free, capable of bearing the weight of pastoral responsibilities. They need to be educated to love the truth, to be loyal, to respect every person, to have a sense of justice, to be true to their word, to be genuinely compassionate, to be men of integrity and, especially, to be balanced in judgment and behavior. (PDV §43)

The need for this human authenticity is evident. An article in *Atlantic Monthly* (April 2001) refers to the young people of our country as "the future workaholics of America." They become too busy to be engaged in anything beyond the realization of their own self-centered concerns. Marriage, if not romance, is put off until their careers are on track. Higher education is a means, not an end—a complaint frequently on the lips of professors and administrators of American colleges and universities. The upwardly mobile dream world of our talented young adults risks becoming little more than empty compulsions and useless competitiveness. In the midst of such a world, a priest, as a fully human and integrated person, should be able to say with conviction: "Stop, look, listen, and take the time to be!"

Priests need a mature capacity to relate to others. As the Pope says again, "This is truly fundamental for a person who is called to be responsible for a community and to be a 'man of communion.'" Such a person cannot be arrogant or quarrelsome; he must be affable, sincere, generous, and ready to serve. The Pope's letter notes that people today are often caught in situations of isolation and loneliness and trapped by poverty and joblessness. To meet those who feel hopeless, extend affection to them,

"We must be listeners, listeners to the Word, listeners to the lives of people, listeners to what the culture is saying. To hear the Word and hear the lives of people requires not only one-to-one experiences. It requires reading—reading that helps us understand the Scriptures and the teaching of the church, reading (e.g., good novels or biographies) that helps us understand what people are going through, and reading that helps us understand the culture." (Murnion 1999, 12)

and help them to find a path to life is "one of the most eloquent signs and one of the most effective ways of transmitting the Gospel message" (*PDV* §43).

Priests also need the rewards and commitment of friendship. Friendship is a reality that bestows great riches and makes great demands. As committed celibate adults, priests must constantly respect the choice that they have publicly made to remain chaste. The powerful emotions that accompany deep friendship sometimes tempt the best of men to violate or compromise their commitment to chastity. Yet the safeguards of prayer, spiritual direction, and trusting openness in peer support groups can protect priests from losing perspective and breaking their vows. The toil of friendship (and deep and lasting friendships are a kind of toil) is essential to a healthy authentic life. Friendship teaches us as nothing else can that ultimately celibacy is not about renouncing love, but precisely about imitating the universal love of the one whose disciple we are, Jesus Christ.

We will have more to say about friendship and priestly affective development in coming chapters. The full humanity of the priest is meant to be a model and a norm for the attitudes and zeal of his pastoral associates and his people. He is someone who both leads and serves, challenges and supports, out of the strength of personality that comes from self-care and responsible growth.

(6) Prophet. The Catholic priest brings God's Word into dialogue with his own life and the life of his people. The most essential way in which this prophetic work is done is through preaching. The Sunday homily presupposes faith and is meant to lead the liturgical gathering from the Word of God to real engagement with the continuing incarnation of God's mercy in their lives. As a work of faith, the homily is an act of interpretation of the world and of our responsibility in it.

"The preacher is a Christian specially charged with sharing the Christian vision of the world as the creation of a loving God. . . . When one hears and accepts this vision of the world, this way of interpreting reality, a response is required" (*FIYH* §§46–47). The preacher's task is formidable. He must speak from the Scriptures, knowing them to be God's living word, with the understanding that his mission is to send the assembly forth "to love and serve the Lord." "We have to hear these texts as real words addressed to real people" (*FIYH* §53). What is the human situation to which

> "Basically the test of any friendship is the truth of the love. Celibate love has its own characteristics: it is the love of 'two solitudes,' who love each other for their mutual growth. There are no strings attached, no exclusivity or possessiveness." (*SR* 33)

> "Authentic prophecy in the biblical sense means that the prophet incarnates his message in his own personality. His communication of the 'prophetic word' to others is simply a transparency of what he is. The prophet of peace to the world is first a man of peace in himself." (*SR* 19)

> "A new possibility opens up to him because he experiences the joy of discovering the living Christ working in his midst. The people indeed become the Christ who serves the priest in a way that complements the priest's ministry of Christ to them."(*SR* 16)

the Word of God must speak here and now? The answer to that question is the beginning of prophecy.

There is a wider prophetic call to which priests must be attentive as well. It is the heritage of Catholic social teaching. The ideological and generational divisions among our Catholic people make it a sensitive matter to preach about social justice. Today one of the great social issues in our country is the huge and growing gap between the very wealthy and the very poor. We are unlikely to have many of the very poor in our Sunday congregations, although we often do have many of the affluent. No one likes to be the bearer of what will seem like bad news to others. Yet we have a strong, objective, and clear tradition of Catholic social teaching going back to the great encyclical of Pope Leo XIII, *Rerum Novarum,* published in May of 1891.

In *A Century of Social Teaching,* the U.S. bishops summarized the Gospel mandate for social justice as follows: "Our faith calls us to work for justice; to serve those in need; to pursue peace; and to defend the life, dignity, and rights of all our sisters and brothers. This is the call of Jesus, the challenge of the prophets, and the living tradition of our Church" (*CST* 1). The most obvious way in which the priest/pastor fulfills this role of prophet is by disseminating the excellent pastoral statements on social issues and political responsibilities published by the United States Conference of Catholic Bishops. The neglect of this kind of social teaching is perhaps attributable to the busy lives of pastors, their lack of special training in politics and economics, and the unfamiliarity or hostility on the part of many of our people to being challenged about social issues on Sunday mornings. Yet in our changing Church, where ethnic and economic minorities are becoming the most vital elements of many dioceses, the failure to address issues of social justice should not continue.

Beyond their preaching, priests need to be advocates of justice for the poor and the underprivileged. Both the work of parish justice programs and the leadership for them may have to be delegated to other responsible parties. But the pastor's neglect of this area altogether would be a mistake.

Finally, the priest should be a strong and conscientious personality. He should express responsible autonomy toward both ecclesiastical and civil authority. He should be a true disciple of Christ. This takes courage: it is not easy to stand up to a bishop or a mayor when the

"Priests who exercise a special prophetic role in the Church need special support from their fellow priests. The prophet begins as one voice and usually remains part of a minority. Those in high places in state and church are not likely to listen to this accusing voice." (*SR* 35)

"In a society that has inherited a taste for violence and war and a history of racial, ethnic and credal injustice; in a society whose institutions reek with racism and discrimination, priests must speak out forthrightly and boldly, and authoritatively lead their people to reject these destructive patterns of thought and behavior." (*SR* 19)

need arises to bring attention to issues of justice seen from the eyes of grass roots responsibility. He can also offer leadership and encouragement to others who take initiatives for justice and peace within the parish and the larger community by the clarity of his own convictions.

THE IDEA OF COMPREHENSIVE MINISTRY

This effort to articulate the multiple roles of priests in terms of these categories of vicar, bearer of the mystery, spiritual personality, pastoral leader, model of human authenticity, and prophet has been what researchers sometimes call "a thought experiment." The value of this exercise will be found in your answer to the question, Can you see yourself in these categories? They represent real factors for ministerial excellence for today's priests. They help to translate the theological understanding of Catholic ministerial priesthood as not just cultic, but comprehensive. The exercise of examining these categories will clarify and illuminate the significance of many of the taxing roles that fall upon priests today. And finally, we hope that these insights will help priests to invest their time and energies more wisely in priorities that really count—and that best match their own particular ministerial gifts.

In threading our way through these roles for priests in today's Church, we have seen both the burdens and the blessings of ordained ministry. In light of the paschal mystery of Jesus, the difficulties of these roles can be understood as a clear sharing in the redemptive suffering of the Lord, a dying to selfish interests, and a surrender to the Spirit's power in the midst of our struggles. We can see as well the force of the resurrection of Christ shining through the promise and achievements of ordained ministry. Priestly life is an invitation to a lifelong conversion to growth in generosity and holiness as disciples of Jesus. In chapter 5 we examine that lifelong conversion and the calls to transformation that it offers us.

Agenda for Personal and Group Reflection

QUESTIONS FOR THE INDIVIDUAL PRIEST

1. What is my assessment of my own pastoral situation: Am I caught in between people at the extremes, or am

I lucky to have a moderate and reasonable pastoral clientele?

2. Realistically do I experience solidarity and support from my fellow priests? From my bishop? What additional support would I like to see?

3. Am I committed to personal growth in my own adult faith development through regular reading and educational workshops?

4. Take an audit: Do I know as much as I should about the nuts and bolts of parish administration? Can/should I delegate some of it to others?

5. What does the criterion of being a prophet—a spokesman for God's living word—mean for my preaching? Am I willing to try to be a prophet?

6. What has been most helpful in seeing these six complementary roles of contemporary priesthood laid out side by side?

QUESTIONS FOR GROUP DISCUSSION

1. Do all six roles describing "comprehensive" priestly ministry make sense to you?

2. How have the actions of the U.S. bishops (and of our own bishop in particular) in response to the scandal of sexual abuse affected our relationship to our ordinary and to our presbyterate?

3. How can we promote adult faith formation? Isn't it really essential for a fully functioning Catholic parish? Where are we failing?

4. What are the most effective means being used in our area to attract "seekers" to our parishes? How can we engage our people to help us in this evangelizing hospitality?

5. Does our diocese offer workshops in skills for pastoral administration that can help priests learn how to run a parish better?

6. Have we figured out how to share Catholic social teaching with our people? In the light of Catholic social teaching's importance for our people's apostolic role in the marketplace, how can we get its message through to them more realistically?

Chapter Five

Transformation through Discipleship

The call to ordination as a priest is a call to stretch oneself, to reach toward a new level of generosity and maturity. What draws Christians to desire a life of ordained ministry varies from case to case. Some are initially attracted by the religious character of liturgical celebration and its beauty, others are moved by the dream of preaching a powerful word, still others by the idea of leading a community toward unity. But however priests originally hear their call and imagine their ministry, they all must recognize that the life itself will mold and shape them. What are important ways in which this transformation takes place in the life of any priest?

THE NEED FOR HUMAN FORMATION

Pope John Paul II's apostolic exhortation, *Pastores Dabo Vobis,* affirms the strong human qualities that are necessary for an authentic personality as well as for effective ministry. These qualities lead people to become "balanced, strong, and free." They require education to love the truth, to respect every person, to have a sense of justice, integrity, and good judgment. This means putting aside arrogance, quarrelsomeness, and self-righteousness and becoming affable and hospitable, while remaining prudent and discreet. Many of those we serve frequently feel trapped in difficult life situations and loneliness and yearn for community support. Priests are called to become significant factors in transmitting the gospel message to those who hunger for love.

Priests are called especially today to be affectively generous and outgoing, available and compassionate for people in a troubled world. Life is incomprehensible for people who don't encounter love in their lives. To exercise leadership in building communities of love, priests need exceptional human maturity and a secure freedom. "Freedom requires the person to be truly master of himself, determined to fight and overcome . . . selfishness and individualism" (*PDV* §44). This theme of freedom as self-mastery is at the heart of the matter. We struggle to know ourselves and to lead ourselves toward our ideals despite pressures to give in to pure self-interest.

A framing metaphor for the life and ministry of priests can be taken from the story of Jacob in the book of Genesis (32:23ff.). On his return to the land of Canaan, Jacob sent his wives and his retinue across the ford of the Jabbok, and then he was left alone, "and a man wrestled with him until daybreak. When the man saw that he did not prevail against Jacob, he struck him on the hip socket" (vv. 24-25). This well-known story of Jacob's wrestling with an angel symbolizes the need for each person to struggle with himself in order to become free and responsible. In the Church of Saint-Sulpice in Paris, there is a bigger than life painting by Delacroix which evokes the powerful experience of Jacob in the Genesis story. The heavenly figure looks overwhelming even to the strong and burly Jacob. Like Jacob, we meet and wrestle with God in the midst of our own journeys and in taking our own next steps toward integrity. This spiritual combat is not just an episode in life, but an enduring dimension of life.

For example, each bishop or priest will wrestle with a variety of ambiguities in his life. What has called us out on this public journey of discipleship and leadership—a hunger for self-esteem and social recognition or a surrender to divine love and a compassionate heart? What moves us on to build the life-giving relationships that keep us going—our spontaneous attraction to those who flatter our sense of well-being, or a faithfulness to those who share our values? What keeps us going on the path of gospel service—an overdose of activities, winning us gratitude and approval, or a balanced regime of prayer, study, community, and ministry? These inevitable questions haunt us as we strive to do the work of ministry and to keep on growing. No one escapes these challenges, but many of us fail to look them straight in the eye.

This life of idealism and spiritual privilege requires a lifetime of fine tuning because certain factors are developmental in nature. Different challenges arise at different points in the spiritual journey. Generalizing, the recently ordained almost always struggle with the surprise, the disappointment, or the burden of discovering that their role or status is not sufficient to carry the day when others in their community disagree and have other ideas. Those in midlife often find themselves frustrated by norms coming down from above (whether from the Vatican or from the chancery): "If only the authorities could see things from my perspective!" Priests aging in ministry today can be frustrated or heartbroken at recognizing that those who share their experience of and enthusiasm for the yeasty days of Vatican II and its aftermath are fewer and fewer in number. These are but a few of the challenges that are linked to the changing circumstances of human lives given over to the service of the Gospel. Many others could be described as well. It seems to be part of the situation of ordained ministry today to find ourselves "in the middle," caught between our own hopes and other people's expectations. What is this strange life really all about?

> "[Ongoing formation] is the continuing [lifelong] integration of priestly identity and functions or service for the sake of mission and communion with Christ and the Church." (*OFP* 11)

IDENTITY AND GENERATIVITY

For years, the question of priestly identity has been a concern of bishops and priests. Pope John Paul II even speaks of emerging "from the crisis of priestly identity" (*PDV* §11). The theme of identity, a term coined by the psychologist Erik Erikson, is an important one. But it can be a labyrinth in which we can become hopelessly lost if our search for clarity about the priest's identity loses its connection with what is most fundamental: self-giving service. Too frequently discussions of priestly identity fail to address another theme developed by Erikson, namely, generativity. In a way that might seem incongruous from a strictly psychological point of view, we could say that the identity of the priest is precisely to be generative. That is, the preoccupation of the generative person is to look away from self and security and to look out for the needs and well-being of others.

Isn't this exactly the meaning of Jesus' important statements in Mark, "Whoever wants to be first must be last of all and servant of all" (9:35), and in Luke, "the

> "The ministry of the priest is sanctifying, not only because the power of God is made perfect in infirmity, but because Christ comes to both minister and recipient in priestly ministrations. The priest as well as the people are touched by the Spirit of God when the Word is proclaimed or the sacraments celebrated." (*SR* 13)

"In fact, priests exist in the world in three principal ways that are interrelated. Priests exist as human beings. They also exist as believing Christians or disciples of Jesus Christ in his Church. Finally, they exist in a unique sacramental mode, as part of the order of presbyters in the Church." (*OFP* 13)

greatest among you must become like the youngest, the leader like the one who serves. . . . I am among you as one who serves"!? (22:26-27). In this regard, *PDV* §12 describes priestly identity as "relational," that is, "to live and work by the power of the Holy Spirit in service of the Church and for the salvation of the world." This is a highly important principle, namely, that the focus of one's concern as a priest is never principally oneself or one's own dignity, but rather the spiritual and social well-being of others. This is exactly the sense in which we insist that priestly identity is precisely about generativity.

The theme of identity in much psychological writing tends to position its reflections at the early stages of identity formation, where a person is just setting out on the journey to adulthood. From this perspective, the focus is upon the quest for identity rather than upon the characteristics of an achieved identity. But we should not confuse the two perspectives. In focusing upon the characteristics of an achieved identity, we largely leave behind the emotional confusion, hesitancy about commitment, and self-preoccupation that pervade feelings of early identity formation. That is why in this context we can point to the generative qualities of an achieved priestly identity.

Erikson considers generativity so important that he sees serious risks for those who fail to develop its characteristics. He calls the failure to develop generativity "stagnation." When adults fail to orient their lives toward creativity, productivity, or concern for the next generation, there is a kind of shutting down of psychic life. Instead of caring about the future of society and the needs of others, such individuals who do not develop generativity become self-focused, indulging their interests in themselves almost as if they were their own child and the sole object of their loving concern. In such situations they often develop a destructive streak leading to cynicism and negativity.

"As a general rule both psychological and spiritual growth occur best in the atmosphere of a loving community where warm human relationships with one's peers and those in authority manifest a certain fullness of life. In such a community love breaks down defenses, allows each person to be himself, and begets the return of love." (*SR* 27)

There will be temptations to some kind of negativity in lives that are filled with challenges and frustration, like the life of any priest or bishop. One of the great themes of *The Spiritual Renewal of the American Priesthood* was its repeated reminder that no individual can or should try to make this journey of generosity and suffering all alone. Each priest and bishop needs and deserves privileged friendships that provide possibilities for sharing their pain, putting their struggles in perspective, and reviving their theological and spiritual motivation in exchanges of mutual trust and support. Moving beyond psychology, we can see that the self-sacrifice, patience, and dedication of generativity are the very substance of the paschal mystery in our lives.

The Toil and Blessing of Friendship

The life of a priest is one of high idealism marked by almost indescribable demands. It is attractive for many reasons, running the gamut from a high social profile and public status to the promise of privileged intimacy with God. But anyone who imagines that the priestly role and its exercise alone will offer him complete human fulfillment and a stable emotional life is mistaken. All the relevant documents, from the Gospel of John through the documents of Vatican II to the encyclicals of Pope John Paul II, stress emphatically the irreplaceable role of friendship in supporting the ministry of priests.

We are born from relationships, destined to find meaning in life through relationships, and called toward the fulfillment of our existence in a divine relationship. We are always in process toward becoming fuller and more complete persons; and the measure of that fullness and completion is our capacity for love and fidelity. Accepting this fate is often a struggle, especially if relationships in our family of origin were strained or dysfunctional. We all must learn our need for others—for friendship. In some ministerial lives, friendship can make the difference between success or failure, happiness or profound disappointment.

Jesus told his disciples, "I do not call you servants . . . I have called you friends" (John 15:15). In the same place he says, "No one has greater love than this, to lay down one's life for one's friends. You are my friends, if you do what I command you" (John 15:13-14). What God seeks from us is the openness of heart, trust, and mutual self-giving that is the reality of friendship. If we are someone's friend, we are more than an object of interest or a useful helper. We have become part of their very self. Friendship wishes everything good for the friend because it has discovered the reality of love. And real friendship exists when this loving relationship is both mutual and committed.

A classic description of the power of love can be found in these words of Robert Johann:

"Personal relationships abound in the priest's life. They are not neatly structured nor easily identified and their influence upon him and his spirit is not easily discernible. Such relationships . . . comprise all the significant persons in his life—fellow priests of his own residence or the local presbyterate, both superiors and peers, friends among the faithful, religious and lay, of both sexes, friends not of the household of the faith, both clergy and lay, members of his family, all those people of his past and present whom he has come to know in some depth and who thus are the important people in his life. These persons have become part of him and mediate life to him at every level of his existence. They nourish him by their care and concern; they challenge him by their trust and acceptance." (*SR* 25)

There we were, wrapped up with ourselves and lost in a seemingly indifferent world. We had allowed ourselves to become harassed by care and anxiety, absorbed with our immediate preoccupations, oppressed by the bleak business of coping with every day. Then suddenly the veil lifted. Through a chance encounter, an unexpected kindness, the sheer radiance of a loving glance, all the more precious because unhoped-for and unmerited, Being beckoned to us. However momentarily, we caught a glimpse of the world beyond care. We came alive. (Johann 1968, 74)

These lines capture the force that love possesses to rebuild our energies, solace our frazzled nerves, and buttress our self-respect.

We have already said enough to emphasize the pressure of overwork and anxiety in the life of a priest. Priests are "givers" ("oblative" personalities, as some psychologists call the type): individuals who find meaning and satisfaction in helping and healing, offering themselves to save and fix the conflicts and needs that others bring to them. The payoff of such a lifestyle are the rewards of gratitude and admiration (however short-lived the effect of that may be). The risk is great, though. Givers come to think of themselves as worth something only when they're giving—performing, ministering, acting, taking charge. They can feel empty and useless in the silent and solitary periods of their lives. This is why givers have a strong tendency to become workaholics: because I can't get enough of affirmation, I don't dare stop giving, giving, giving. . . .

"Ongoing formation necessarily includes an increasing integration of one's sexuality. As noted previously, sexuality is an energy or passion directed toward connecting, belonging, and giving life. While a celibate commitment is not expressed in genital sexual activity or in an exclusive intimate relationship, the priest remains a sexual person who is expected to develop mature expressions of chaste love and caring." (*OFP* 25)

Only friendship and grace can cut through this oblative syndrome. Friendship is a requisite dimension of mature human development. Erikson, whose ideas we mentioned above, places "intimacy" as a stage between "identity" and "generativity." One learns intimacy by learning to respect and love another not as a useful adjunct for his needs or as an object of fantasy to aggrandize his ego. Intimacy means losing oneself in another, finding another person good and worthy of time and trust. Look again at the words of Robert Johann cited above. They show us that intimacy usually comes into our lives as a surprise. We don't calculate friendship, we discover it or receive it as a gift. This kind of trust and reciprocal caring is a necessity for priestly maturity—for growth into freedom and confidence as a person.

Without retracting in the least this claim for the importance of friendship, we also need to acknowledge that true and faithful friendship is not easy. It requires honesty, patience, and faithfulness. Making time for friends when your days are desperate with overwork and overcommitment means really believing in the importance of this kind of relationship. And even the best of friendships have their ups and downs. It is essential to value friends without idealizing them, to invest time in their company without expecting utopian results. It is also important to recognize that friendship often brings suffering through misunderstanding, disappointments, or emotional and cultural limitations. With all that—despite all that—friendship is an irreplaceable part of human growth.

FRIENDSHIP WITH CHRIST
AS THE BASIS OF CELIBATE LOVE

Vatican II's decree on the training of priests *Optatam Totius* explains that those who take on a likeness to Christ through priestly ordination should understand their relationship to the Lord as that of friends. They need to understand the dynamics of the paschal mystery (dying and rising with Christ in the circumstances of their own lives) so fully that they will be able to introduce the people to whom they minister to this same mystery (8). As friends of Christ, priests need to learn the habits of friendship with Christ—taking time, entrusting secrets, listening patiently, adapting to the ways of the friend. In our human friendships we gradually learn the difference between the "idea" of having a friend and the "reality" of a life enriched by friendship. With Christ, it is altogether too easy to think and talk and imagine that we have a friendship with the Lord, when in fact all we have is an "idea" of friendship.

True friendship with Christ brings us inside the mysteries of the Scriptures that we proclaim and preach. We learn that we are able to go on with Christ despite obstacles, betrayal, rejection, and suffering. Remember Paul's words in First Corinthians: "Think of us in this way, as servants of Christ and stewards of God's mysteries" (4:1). This is the role of the bearer of the mystery (mystagogue) discussed above. We are transformed by our initiation into the mystery of Christ. We are plunged by the grace of our calling into giving ourselves fully to the kingdom of God.

"Man is not always faithful, understanding, forgiving; he fails to anticipate the other's need, to be perceptive of another's hurt, to be grateful for the concern shown him. All human friendship is defective and friends do defect. . . . Moments of pain are inevitable. Sometimes the attrition is so bad that isolation and alienation result, with the feeling sometimes mentioned by older priests, that they do not 'belong' any more. This suffering can truly be configuration to the suffering Christ. The more one loves, the more vulnerable he becomes." (*SR* 28)

Robert Barron links this mystagogical dimension of priesthood to celibacy when he writes:

Celibacy is unreasonable, unnatural, and excessive, which is why it has been chosen, across cultures and throughout history, as one of the ways in which lovers of God have traditionally expressed their love. To try to understand this self-gift or explain it is to miss the point. Not surprisingly, mystagogues, those who have been chosen by the Mystery to speak of the Mystery, see the appropriateness of this excessive stance and lifestyle. (Barron, 1999, 99)

One doesn't have to agree with all of Barron's imagery to agree with him that celibacy is rooted in friendship with Christ, following him in his self-giving and gratuitous love.

"Celibacy is clearly a way of living human sexuality. Clear too: celibacy will become unintelligible when the delicate cultural framework channeling more primitive sexual instincts breaks down. When human sexuality reverts to instinct, celibacy loses meaning." (*Celibacy for the Kingdom* 17)

Celibacy is not a renunciation of love, but a commitment to a universal love. Jesus teaches priests to pray to God as "Abba" and so to see themselves as "brothers" in a new light. In light of the kingdom that Jesus preached, "Whoever does the will of God is my brother and sister and mother" (Mark 3:35). If priests give up a nuclear family of their own, they gain another family—the family of faith. As mystagogues who "dispense" the mysteries of Christ in their ministry, priests as friends of Christ learn the ways of a pastoral intimacy that can touch the deepest human hurts and human hungers. Through their friendship with Christ and their fidelity to their own friends, priests learn how their celibacy is not a denial of sexuality, but a specific way of molding and shaping it.

Realistic Idealism

In reading the documents about priestly formation, from the Second Vatican Council down to the encyclicals of Pope John Paul II, it is wrong to suppose that a perfectly stable human development must be in place before the life of ministry may begin. A number of misconceptions can flow from this mistake: a nominalism that imagines that ideal qualities must be in place simply because someone has been ordained, or a guilty defeatism that lives with the grinding anxiety of knowing that one lacks these ideal qualities, or an arrogance that imagines the individual as a special case exempt from the demands placed on lesser beings. So we should be clear. We are trying to talk realistically about a life penetrated with idealism. We likewise acknowledge the important role of forgiveness and reconciliation for our failures along the way.

Priesthood is a lifetime of transformation through discipleship. Demanding as it is, ordained ministry, according to the tradition we have received from the Church's living experience, requires striving toward this Christ-like self-giving. But this has to be understood as a journey toward integrity. A classmate remarked to a fellow seminarian in the procession of their ordination Mass, "Remember, this is a sacrament, not a miracle!" That's good advice for each of us.

Many priests have been touched by the phrase "wounded healer," the title of an enduringly helpful book by Henri Nouwen. The idea is clear enough: our own woundedness builds a bridge and provides the instrument for our reaching out to the woundedness of others. As 1 Peter summarizes our redemption in Christ with the phrase, "By his wounds you have been healed" (2:24), so also as friends of Christ and stewards of his mysteries, others may be healed by our wounds. God's use of our actions and our gifts is not limited to our calculated or preconceived notions of how we might be effective.

Bishops are challenged to bring together and oversee the gifts in ministry of "wounded healers," knowing full well the awesome challenge that their priests face. Priests' lives are generally overstressed. As Michael Himes has put it, "The presbyterate has been a jack-of-all-trades ministry. . . . As a job description, it is impossible" (Himes 1999, 45).

We have never had a team of supermen as the Church's pastoral leaders. From the beginning we had a leader who had denied his Master, disciples who fled from the Cross, and an apostle who had persecuted the early Church out of fundamentalistic zeal—and the centuries did not change the pattern essentially. Mistakes and renewal, betrayal and conversion—all this has been the pattern of persevering discipleship. Our honesty in facing up to that, and to the consequences of a life of ongoing *growth* and *becoming* as disciples, is at the heart of priestly ministry.

"Role expectations among the clergy leave many feeling trapped, overworked, frustrated and with a sense of little or no time for themselves. The continuing shortage of clergy casts its shadow on both present ministry and future hopes." Priestly Life and Ministry Committee, *Origins* 18 (1989) 500

CHALLENGES FOR PRIESTLY DEVELOPMENT

Recent research conducted by Dean Hoge and his associates has identified some concrete challenges that express

"He needed a chief to guide his
    people, so he chose an old
    man: and Abraham got up;
He needed a Rock to build his
    Church upon, so he chose
    the one who denied him:
    and Peter got up.
He needed a face to show us
    his love, so he chose a
    prostitute: none other than
    Mary Magdalen.
He needed a witness to
    broadcast his message, so
    he chose the one who had
    persecuted him: that was
    Paul of Tarsus.
He still needs someone to
    gather his people together:
    and he has chosen you—
Even if you're afraid, can't you
    still give yourself?" (Bernard
    Bonvin, *Dieu silence, Dieu
    présence*, 158–59; trans.
    Philibert)

the disappointment and wounds of U.S. priests over the last few years. Three concerns capture the principal anxieties of those surveyed in this research. The first issue has to do with trust, communication, and meaningful relationships between diocesan priests and their bishops, and between religious priests and their superiors. While Hoge's research data collected before January 2002 does not tell us this, we can reasonably presume that the bishops' response to the sexual abuse scandals has further aggravated the feeling of alienation between priests and bishops, and between clerical religious and their superiors. Another aspect of the relationship between bishops and priests is priests' disappointment that they have no say now in who is going to be called to become their bishop. This was not always the case. One of our deepest hopes and expectations for this document is that it will be able to serve as an instrument for genuine dialogue and healing conversation between priests and their ordinaries.

A second strong concern of priests discovered by the research was the extent of loneliness felt by the priests in the survey—most notably among the recently ordained. They feel overextended, underprepared, and very much alone. In one of our listening sessions, our writing committee met with three recently ordained men who are talented and succeeding with large pastoral responsibilities. We were surprised and somewhat shaken to hear the first of them tell us: "I wonder how long I can keep doing this in the way I'm doing it. How viable is this life for me?" He spoke of how draining it is for him to pour himself out without recognition from his bishop or his peers. He finds himself asking at times: "Who gives a damn?"

The second of the three told us: "Do we have enough preparation to face the real world—things like budgets, administration, and the financial problems of a parish? I find myself both emotionally and intellectually overwhelmed." He went on to say that he needs more help with practical things. Who can he talk to? Who can he call? The technical side of this is one thing, but the emotional side is another—and that underlines the discussion about friendship above.

The third recently ordained priest told us:

I'm forced to do lots of different things, but I don't know how well. We are in the midst of a massive cultural shift, and I wonder how many people are willing to move into a new pastoral re-

ality, that is, face up to the facts of multiculturalism, generational change, and the need for evangelization. I worry that all this will make me numb to the things I love. I worry that I don't have the time, energy, or desire to pray.

Here are men who love their ministry, who love to preach and to lead their people in sacramental life. But they are being quickly exhausted by patterns of over-work without being sufficiently replenished by spiritual practices.

We find similar anxieties expressed by some older priests who minister to multiple parishes. They spoke of their deep concern for the people they serve and for their own well-being. One of these priests explained:

I feel real anxiety about whether I'm going to be able to pre-serve emotional connection to the people if my ministry becomes more narrow and more spread-out. I need to feel like I know people, their joys, and their challenges. I enjoy preaching and dealing with large groups, but a lot of my energy comes from working with individuals and families, counseling and forming relationships. I fear that won't be possible.

Another said: "I'm not part of the communities I minister sacramentally in. We have five sisters who live and work in three counties. And I'm running instead of relating" (*Priestless Parishes* 1991, 10).

Priests' feelings of loneliness are closely connected to overwork and to disappointment at having to revise their expectations for ministry. The "circuit rider" priest plays an essential role in some rural dioceses, but it is often a difficult one precisely because he is unable to do the spiritual and liturgical formation of the people for whom he celebrates. He just can't be there most of the time. This calls for a close spirit of collaboration between the priest—as sacramental minister—and the deacon, religious, or lay pastoral administrator. And that calls for special understanding and generosity—a style of colleague-ship for which most priests have not been adequately prepared

Finally, a third issue arising out of the new research on priests lifts up the need for seminaries to focus more realistically on spiritual development. Hoge and Wenger cite a 32-year-old priest who says, "Teach the men how to pray. Teach them what it is, and I don't want to sound melodramatic, but teach them to learn how to die to

"If sacramental experience deteriorates, it's hard to see what value there is for people to remain Catholic. They can get word services elsewhere. Combining this with the impression that the status quo's preservation means more to the institutional church than the needs of the people, there could be a morale problem that transcends that of priests." (*Priestless Parishes* 1991, 10)

themselves"(Hoge and Wenger 2003, 135). A 42-year-old diocesan priest adds, "from what I've witnessed from priests since I've been out here . . . priests that tend to fail, to burn out, tend to be priests who neglect their prayer" (Hoge and Wenger 2003, 136) An older priest, ordained in 1972, observed:

How do you make a person realize the importance of prayer and its connection to ministry before you're really involved in ministry? Lay people want to see priests who are in love with the Lord, have a passion for God, and they want guys to share their passion for God. And you're only going to get that passion as you see the need for prayer and ministry. (Hoge and Wenger 2003, 136)

"The priest is an agent of reconciliation primarily by being a man reconciled in himself through his own participation in the paschal mystery. This is the specific way in which he serves mankind. His exercise of ministry contributes to this personal reconciliation in himself by effecting a continuing self-transformation, a deeper self-understanding whereby he becomes more conformed to the image of the Son (Rom 8:29) and more deeply involved in the process of dying and rising with Christ." (*SR* 18)

How is it possible for us to remain realistic about priestly spiritual ideals in the face of these daunting expectations? Ministry for these men converges with the all too real emergencies of our moment in history. How does priestly idealism cope with the troubled climate created by clerical sexual abuse, a growing priest shortage, the needs of multicultural communities lacking adequately trained ministers, and the growing expectations for ordained ministry—at the same time that the workforce is spread thinner and thinner? We trust that you are going to ask these questions of one another, with your bishop or major superior, honestly, creatively, and courageously.

REASONS TO BE HOPEFUL

Pope John Paul II lays out the challenge for a priest's human development in these terms: "In order that his ministry may be humanly as credible and acceptable as possible, it is important that the priest should mold his human personality in such a way that it becomes a bridge and not an obstacle for others in their meeting with Jesus Christ" (*PDV* §43). If a priest's personality is to be a bridge rather than a barrier, then two aspects of human development must be faced.

First, what is given to a person in terms of gifts, talents, and endowments must be owned and affirmed; while, secondly, what is lacking in terms of weakness, limitations, and shortcomings, must be accepted with humility and honesty. Healthy and happy priests are realistically oriented, spontaneous, accepting of themselves and others. They are problem solvers, autonomous and independent, creative, humorous, nonconforming, positive, and secure. If they function well, they are risk takers, confident and enthusiastic, integrated and congruent, self-directive and self-actualizing. They are people with high self-esteem who generally accept the way life treats them. They are active participants rather than reactive receptors. Far from fearing change, they welcome it and know that it is an inescapable part of life.

That is not to say that leaving one assignment to go to another isn't painful, or that transitions are easily made. These and other challenges, like having to work with difficult parish leaders, are going to be a part of life. Healthy priests have made the decision to embrace challenges and change, and to see them as being life giving. They have a sense of unity and balance in their lives.

Having a sense of balance means keeping perspective on life and maintaining a realistic sense about complex demands. Healthy priests make wise choices about how to use their time in order to be free and responsible. They are able to see the whole picture without losing touch with the details. Their honesty enables them to keep a sense of vision and a passion for mission. Happy priests enjoy being accountable to others—superiors, colleagues— and want others to be the same with them. Well-adjusted priests have learned to find support and meet their needs for intimacy in a variety of ways. They look to family, to support groups, as well as to lay people and religious women and men with whom they form friendships and close relationships.

These priests are believers in God and in themselves. They believe that God speaks to them in the language of experience. Accordingly, they believe that what they're doing is a worthwhile way to spend their lives. They believe that the Good News of the Gospel is an important message for the world, and that God has called them to work for and to wait for the coming of the kingdom in God's good time.

In the meantime, they continue their ministry of preaching Sunday after Sunday and day after day even when they may not understand *how* God's action will come about. Deep down, they believe that God loves them, and this makes all the difference in the world. They don't ask, "What would Jesus do?" They strive in their lives to speak in the words of Jesus and to model their lives on Jesus as their "pioneer and perfecter of our faith" (Heb 12:2). But their lives are not so much an imitation

"The rewards more than balance the effort demanded. For those priests who conceive of their ministerial relationship in terms of a spiritual director of ministries in the Church, who see themselves as stimulators of the communion process, the ministry itself offers a powerful stimulus for personal spiritual growth." (*SR* 17)

of Jesus as a vital interiorizing of Jesus. The paschal mystery is their starting point for theological reflection, preaching, and prayer. It is likewise the confirmation of what they believe about discipleship.

To maintain their relationship with Jesus at the center of their lives, they engage in spiritual practices that permit them to recognize and respond to the Holy Spirit. The building blocks of this spirituality are prayer, Scripture, and the celebration of the sacred liturgy. Effective and happy priests practice the constant awareness of the presence of God in their lives. They believe that God is actively involved in their lives and ministry. When they engage in ministry, they likewise believe that God is working through them, and as a result of doing ministry to others, they receive back tenfold in return.

Their attentive listening is important for a life-giving ministry. From the people they serve they hear a confirmation of the impact that they have in their lives. They have found what it means to live a generative life. They have discovered the meaning of having life in abundance—and giving the gift away.

Recent research conducted by Dean Hoge and his associates as well as the 2002 national survey of priests by the *Los Angeles Times* show that the great majority of priests find their lives fulfilling and meaningful, and they are grateful for their vocations to priestly life. Many are concerned about the demands that present circumstances place on them and about loneliness. And some of them quite explicitly acknowledge their need for more structure in their spiritual practices. So we will try to describe what these practices of spirituality look like in the life of a busy priest. That is what we turn to next.

"I have found the priesthood to be such an enormously fulfilling and happy life that I couldn't imagine any alternative for me. So I can't really take any credit for being committed to my life; it has been such a wonderful experience not only to be creative but to have the opportunity to carry out my ideas." (William J. Bausch in Friedl and Reynolds 1997, 107)

Agenda for Personal and Group Reflection

QUESTIONS FOR THE INDIVIDUAL PRIEST

1. Where do I find myself caught between my own hopes and other people's expectations?

2. Can I see the difference between the quest for identity and an achieved identity? Does this clarification give me a better focus on my own feelings?

3. Who are my friends? Do I have someone who really knows me and whose care sees me through my self-doubts and failures?

4. Am I caught in the cycle of being always a "giver" in search of emotional rewards? Am I a workaholic? How can I learn better to "receive"?

5. How do I describe the ways that Christ's universal love takes shape in me? What thoughts and words represent my heart's spontaneous movements? Do I recognize love and celibacy as practically linked in the way I live my priesthood?

6. How am I a "wounded healer"? Can I see God using the weakness in my life to gain the weak for the gospel? (cf. 1 Cor 9:22).

QUESTIONS FOR GROUP REFLECTION

1. How do we assess the morale of our local presbyterate in terms of participation in diocesan programs for priests, *esprit de corps* among the gathered priests, and regularity of contact for social support?

2. Does looking at the identity of the priest as "generative" shift questions about priestly identity into a wider frame of reference than we usually take? Why is that the case?

3. Does this diocese (or religious congregation) have a structure in place for mentoring the recently ordained and those coming from other cultures? Would better mentoring enhance diocesan life (or the ministries of religious institutes)? How?

4. Celibacy is linked to generativity and is expressive of our friendship with Christ. Let's talk about how this really works in our lives. How do we do it?

5. What are the forces that create overwork and frustration among us? Can we share ideas, resources, and energies in ways that will make it better?

6. What work of reconciliation does our diocese need at this time—between bishops and priests, between priests and priests, and between clergy and laity? How should we go about initiating the ministry of reconciliation?

Chapter Six

The Practices of the Spiritual Life

God is eager to call all priests into a fuller life of prayer.
Catholic priests have a long tradition of spiritual practices
designed to open them to the transforming power of
grace. Here is a picture of those practices becoming a
natural part of the rhythm of a priest's life.

Remembering the story from the first book of Samuel
of the child Samuel in the house of Heli the high priest
(1 Sam 3:1-10), let's imagine a typical presbyter named
Sam. Sam, like the boy Samuel, is someone who has
learned to say at the appropriate times, "Speak, LORD, for
your servant is listening" (1 Sam 3:9). This practice of listening is one piece of the warning that we used to see at
railroad crossings: "Stop, Look, and Listen!"

In Sam's life, however, railroad crossings aren't the
issue, but rather the typical thresholds that he crosses
every day. He is learning to listen for God's voice as he
moves between sleeping and waking, action and contemplation, group activity and solitary work, ministry and
study, giving and opening up to receive, effort and rest.
Listening to the voice of God transformed Samuel from a
generous and pious child, who was ready to give his life
to religious service, into an astute prophetic judge who
was able to act authoritatively at God's direction. He became someone who could discern God's will.

The gift of spiritual discernment entails keeping a
unified focus on the whole of life, seeing it all as gift and
encounter. The enemy of such spiritual discernment is
compartmentalizing life into packages, some of which are
sacred and others secular, some dramatically inspirational
and others prosaically commonplace. This is how ministers get burned out. They pour all their energies into giving, performing sacred rites, trying to help, and to fulfill a

million expectations, and then dropping over with exhaustion—too tired to read, study, rest, pray, or socialize.

When we package life into sacred modules and secular respites, usually two things happen. First, we get so busy that we can't realistically balance work and rest, and the result is workaholism. Second, our minds and hearts become so weary that the only thing we resort to for a break is passive absorption of the media, most of all television. As a result we do not take the time for study, nourishing conversation, restorative exercise, and thoughtful reflection before the next round of performing more sacred modules—sacramental or pastoral or administrative. Eventually we find our pastoral contribution becoming thin and unsatisfying.

Perhaps we need to post over our doorways, our desks, and our dashboards signs, like the crossed white arms at rural railroad track junctions, to remind us to "Stop, Look, and Listen." *Stop:* give yourself a chance to feel what has happened in the past hour's sacramental rite or pastoral conversation or staff meeting. *Look:* see if you can perceive how God has been present in this hour and, above all, present to others through you. *Listen:* how is God speaking to you in these events—to affirm your call to stand in for God, to awaken you to your community's life and gifts, and to direct you back to Scripture and theological reflection?

It is noteworthy that professionals like doctors, lawyers, nurses, and psychologists are obliged by law to make summary records of what transpires in a given case after an interaction with a patient or a client. "What happened? Then what happened next? And what happened to me?" Many priests learned how to do this kind of assessment during their CPE programs. It was meant to develop an insightful habit that would endure throughout their lives of ministry. Stop. Look. Listen.

Sam has gradually learned his lessons. He has decided that he wants a balanced life. He enjoys being able to help, but he knows that he also needs to be helped. His greatest pleasure comes from serving through giving, but he has learned that he must also be nourished himself if he is to persevere. After crash landings into fatigue, loneliness, and mild depression, Sam has set up a rhythm in his life of giving and receiving, acting and waiting. Let's follow him through a day of his life as a priest and see how he juggles his multiple responsibilities.

6:00 A.M. The alarm clock buzzes. He has been resting, half-awake for half an hour. Now the time has come

"I must experience Jesus Christ. Jesus is the center of my life: Neither culture, nor ministry, nor life together, nor even prayer itself is my spiritual life. The Lord is my life, and until I meet him on one or all of the concentric circles [of my life], I have not become a man of the Spirit. It is not enough to experience prayer or people or ministry. I must experience him." (*SR* 57)

to get up. As he accepts the new day and its routine with its surprises and challenges, he says quite simply, "Hello, God—thanks for giving me life, another day, the strength and energy of my body, the hope and passion in my heart. I am yours." The first few moments of the day unfold in silence—in a vague, loving act of obedience that can't be put into words. This may only last two or three minutes, but they are two or three important minutes that consign his day to God's will.

Before heading for the bathroom and the shower, Sam repeats a prayer he wrote himself a few years ago—a morning offering. "Source of all Being, loving God, I offer you my life this day through Jesus in the power of his Spirit. Accept all my prayers, works, joys, and sufferings in union with the dying and rising of my Savior. Give me patience, joy, and understanding in the hours of this day that I now receive as a gift from you. Glory to you, loving God: Father, Son, and Holy Spirit."

6:30 A.M. Sam takes a quick cup of coffee, glances at the headlines, and then settles down in his prayer space. He lights a candle in front of an icon that speaks to his heart. This is one of the ways in which he feels God taking the initiative in his prayer. These next twenty-five minutes are God's time. He prays the Jesus Prayer repeatedly: "Jesus . . . Mercy . . . !" He tries to listen, to allow his breathing, his physical presence, and his love to be both the prayer he says and the prayer God wants the Holy Spirit to pray within him. Twenty-five minutes go by pretty quickly.

"For all who are guided by the Spirit of God are children of God. For you did not receive a spirit of slavery to fall back into fear, but you have received a spirit of adoption. When we cry 'Abba! Father!' it is that very Spirit bearing witness with our Spirit that we are children of God." (Rom 8:14-16)

7:30 A.M. After breakfast and some time with the newspaper and the radio news, Sam prays Morning Prayer and gets ready for an 8:00 A.M. Mass in church. He presides at the morning Mass with about thirty weekday regulars. He preaches a four-minute homily on one point, inviting his people to welcome God's Word into their hearts. He especially loves the physical act of communicating the assembly: "The body of Christ." He remembers that he has just prayed in the Eucharistic Prayer, "May your Holy Spirit make us one body, one spirit in Christ." He wants them all to know this and to feel the spiritual joy that is their unity with one another and with God.

After greeting some of the folks who linger after Mass and handing over the sacristy clean-up to a lay assistant, Sam takes five minutes or so for thanksgiving. Without need for words, he hands over the joys and the hopes of his people to God. He asks for the grace to be led by the Spirit. A busy day is about to begin.

9:15 A.M. Sam has a meeting at 10:00, so he has about 45 minutes to go back and reread the Lectionary for next Sunday. He looks at a couple of translations of the gospel for those Masses. Sometimes a different wording will break open the meaning of the Sunday Scriptures for him. He tries to sketch out a paraphrase of the gospel story, asking: "What is Jesus saying to us? What is he saying to this parish and our present circumstances?" "Dear God, let me make your word a living word. Let me speak for you. I'm trying to listen," prays Sam.

Last Monday when he came in from Mass there was a note from the ushers about a leak in the roof. That led to half a dozen phone calls and additional hours of work. Today, no rain, no leaks. The doorbell rings.

"[E]xperience continues to support the traditional conviction that the man who prays on the job is also the man who enters his room and prays to the Father in secret, who takes time out to be alone with the Lord, who gains and gives strength to his brothers in the priesthood by praying together with them."

(*SR* 48)

10 A.M. to 12 noon. Sam receives a middle-aged woman whose mother just died in a nursing home. He listens to the story of the dead woman's life, tries to console her daughter, and makes arrangements for the wake service (which the parish bereavement committee will direct) and the funeral Mass. Before his visitor leaves, Sam takes her hand and prays with her, briefly handing her family over to God—thinking of other members of the family, the youngsters left behind by this dead grandmother, and her many friends in the parish. "May we know you better, Lord, by seeing her enter your circle of eternal life," Sam prays.

Yesterday at this time there was an urgent call for him from the hospital about someone who had just been in an auto accident, and that took up the rest of that morning. Today he now turns to phone messages, mail, and letters until noon. "Lord, be in the midst of all this—somehow," Sam sighs, as he signs and seals his last letter of the morning.

12:15 P.M. Sam welcomes Fr. Andrew Tran, recently assigned to the neighboring parish—a Vietnamese priest ordained this year and new to town. Together they have a simple lunch of soup and sandwiches, a rare opportunity for them both just to be with a priest friend. They talk about their families, their previous lives, and their hopes for their futures as priests. Sam had invited Andrew to take a bike ride for about an hour, and together they ride to a nearby park, where Sam shows Andrew some of his favorite spots to relax. As they bike along, Sam thinks, "Lord, thank you for this refreshing interlude, this beautiful place, this bit of time to enjoy the beautiful world you've given me. Be praised!" Sam wonders if the good feeling of being alive at moments like this is itself a kind of prayer. He hopes so.

2:30 P.M. Sam is back in his office. More visitors, more phone calls, a little more time for the Sunday homily (because he's been thinking about the readings in the back of his mind since earlier that morning)—and soon it's five o'clock. As happens a couple of times a week, today one of the women of the parish has left him a covered dish supper destined for the microwave.

He will have a parish council meeting at 7:30. So at 5:15, he goes over to church, prays Evening Prayer and lingers for a bit of silence after the reading. (On Sunday night, he prays Evening Prayer of the Liturgy of the Hours with members of the parish, but tonight he is on his own.) Then he locks up the church and heads back to the kitchen for supper. The head of the parish council arrives by 7:15, and together they prepare the room for their council meeting.

9:00 P.M. Sam says good-bye to the last departing council member. As he ended the council meeting with a pastoral prayer, he thanked God for these twelve people and the ministries of the parish that they represent—education, social service, development, liturgy, parish events, evangelization, and welcome committee . . . "Lord, give me the wisdom to encourage and support these people, to welcome their dreams and to shape their understanding of your Gospel. Thank you for allowing me to be a brother and father to them."

9:15 P.M. Sam has an hour to relax. Some nights there are programs on TV that he looks forward to seeing. Tonight, however, he's anxious to get back to a novel he began a few days ago. "Stories—stories are so great," he thinks. "Maybe that's why I like being a priest so much: I get to live in so many different stories."

10:30. Sam's ready to turn in. He reviews the day quickly—five minutes in his prayer corner, candle lighted once again. "I give this day to you, Lord. Be the light in their minds, the joy in their hearts, the power in their actions. I did my best. I love you. Thank you. Amen." And off to bed.

A faithful and faith-filled day—one lived in the power of Christ's Spirit. Tiring, replenishing, taxing, joyful. As Sam drifts off to sleep, he almost unconsciously realizes when he was listening and when God was

"Where do I begin the process? The answer lies in my real life, my total experience. This means that human experience is the 'stuff' of spirituality and that under God's grace and enlightened by loving faith I construct my spiritual life out of my interactions on the four levels of existence: my world, my people, my friends, my Lord." (SR 59)

speaking. He is learning to discern the hidden presences of God.

There are skills that make this kind of life possible: active listening (listening to what isn't said, but meant all the same), dynamic silence (knowing God speaks in silences and hears our silences), a humble sense of humor (not taking yourself too seriously), and spiritual direction. Each of these helps Sam to remain faithful to his demanding but rewarding life as a priest.

LEARNING TO LISTEN

Listening is a practice that is needed for good pastoral leadership and for real openness to prayer. Sam has gradually learned over time how important listening is. When he first became pastor, he had trouble getting his parish council to become involved. He had the idea that once he explained his plans for the parish's projects, they would all enthusiastically agree and jump on board. He was surprised and disappointed when he was often met with silence or with what seemed to him to be picky objections to his ideas. He remembers the night that Dave, one of his parishioners, a forty-year-old psychologist who lives in the neighborhood, took him aside and said to him, "Excuse me, Father, but I think I could help you enjoy this a lot better. Could we talk?"

Dave said, "Father Sam, you are our leader, but you are also leading a team of people who have to buy into the vision and the projects that you propose to them. You need to get them more involved. People commit their time and their energies when you involve them in leadership. Think of them as leaders of the parish community, and they will become just that for you."

Dave explained how seldom it is that people feel like they are really listened to in any institution. "Psychologists have come up with an idea called 'active listening' that is very important for a lot of contexts. Leadership in group work is one of those contexts. Let people talk, share their misgivings about an idea, suggest variations or new possibilities, think over the possible consequences—get all that out on the table. It takes time. But it makes the parish council, a staff meeting, or any other group work into a real community. And it generates enthusiasm, loyalty, and generosity."

"If human formation aims to cultivate the humanity of priests so that their humanity is instrumental in communicating Jesus Christ . . . then the general means of such formation are clear. Psychological and sociological self-knowledge, for example, are essential. Cultivating one's capacity for communication as listener and speaker strengthens the capacity for dialogue and communion."
(*OFP* 24–25)

Dave met with Sam a couple of other times, and it helped him understand better how to be a leader. "First make sure you have really heard what someone is saying," Dave urged. "You can try to repeat back to them a paraphrase of what you're hearing. Whatever the issue is, make sure you both understand the idea and feel the emotion behind it before you try to respond to it."

When Sam started putting this into practice, he found that his relationship with the parish council changed dramatically for the better. People who had never spoken up before started joining in and contributing. Others who had never volunteered for follow-up work became involved for the first time. More important, Sam stopped feeling so threatened by the meeting, by the council members, and by possible conflicts or stalemates.

With Dave's help, Sam carried this attitude of active listening over into his pastoral counseling and sacramental preparation work. By listening more, he was able to invite a deeper involvement from people in what he taught them or proposed to them, whether they were in trouble and seeking help, or at a point of approaching the sacraments. Just as important, Sam learned to become less controlling and demanding, and more patient and serene in lots of different ways. All this has spilled over into his prayer. "Am I listening to God any better than I was listening to the parish council before I met Dave?" Sam thought. "It takes a long time to learn this stuff. I want to talk about this with my spiritual director. This could really be important after all."

DYNAMIC SILENCE

More and more at his half hour of daily prayer Sam realized that active listening was helping him to understand what God wanted from him. He remembered the retreat master last year proposing the phrase from Psalm 45, "Be still, and know that I am God!" (v. 10) as an image of prayer. "This phrase was important in the spiritual writings of the Fathers of the Church and in monastic writings," the retreat master said. "God's Word remains active and alive in us long after we have heard or read Sacred Scripture. We have to allow God's Word some time and a chance to unfold inside of us."

This was a good insight for Sam. In Christian prayer, word and silence go together. Recently he read an article

"Prayer begins with listening to God's Word, and the language God speaks is man [sic]. God bespeaks himself fully and completely in the Man, who is Jesus Christ. . . . Our task as listeners, our 'prayer,' is not to look for a message, but to become aware of the Word of the Lord embedded in human reality all about us and to discern the Lord's presence in our midst." (*SR* 52)

in *Celebration* saying how unfortunate it is that we pay so little attention to the liturgy's invitation to pause in silent prayer during the Mass—after the readings, the preaching, the people's communion. The liturgy wants us to express our assent and our readiness for grace with our whole selves at rest before God. Our minds are so flexible and complex, and so often we treat them like computers. We have to relearn how to imagine, feel, love, embrace, and intend with our minds—not just think! The whole Church has to learn again how to pray in silence, as the liturgy asks us to do.

Sam began to see this as linked to what he had learned about active listening. God will speak to our hearts, but not in words. God spoke to Moses on Mount Sinai in thunder and lightening and to Elijah on Mount Horeb in a gentle breeze. God spoke to David in the psalms in the splendors of the starry sky and the beauty of creation, and to Hosea in the lonely silence of the desert. These were great moments of revelation whose content was not new information, but a new formation of awareness and heart. At some point in every earnest Christian's life, that exactly will be the heart of prayer. God is here and speaking, but in God's way, not in mine. Be still and trust—and listen!

God often speaks in silences and hears our silences in return. "That's a hard idea to understand and a harder practice to carry out," Sam realized. But now he understood that nonetheless that's the way the Christian life works. The Gospels go out of their way to remind us of the nights Jesus spent in prayer—much of it surely in just this kind of silence. Dynamic silence.

God speaks in silences, yes; but to people who have already heard his word over and over again. This is not a Buddhist quest for emptiness or flight from the pain of the world. This is a perfectly Christian discipline as old and as authentic as Jesus' own prayer through long nights in communion with his Father. The Word of God, which is the nourishment of Christian prayer, expands within us. No one reading or proclamation of Scripture exhausts its power. No homily or theological passage or spiritual conversation is ever adequate to the fullness of God's Word. Rather God's Word expands and unfolds as light and life, hours later, and most especially in the silence of prayer.

One way this happens is through *lectio divina*—the meditative lingering over the Scriptures as prayer. This ancient practice seeks to hear God's voice speaking through the act of reading the books of the Bible. It teaches us to stop and

"[T]he Spirit helps us in our weakness; for we do not know how to pray as we ought, but that very Spirit intercedes with sighs too deep for words. And God, who searches the heart, knows what is the mind of the Spirit, because the Spirit intercedes for the saints according to the will of God."
(Rom 8:26-27)

"Prayer from this point of view is an act of hope. It is waiting in trustful expectation, in emptiness and openness, knowing that the Lord will visit the one who seeks him."
(*SR* 53)

pause as soon as our heart is touched by the message that God sends in the reading. Little by little we make our way through the text, listening—listening—listening . . . knowing that God will speak. Not in words, perhaps, but in a filling up of the heart with a call, with comfort, with love, and with a new sense of purpose. . . . Sam has discovered that he needs one continuous period of at least twenty minutes a day for prayer that will really sustain him.

"Speak, LORD, for your servant is listening" (1 Sam 3:9). How long it takes to believe that God does just that kind of speaking using the privileged language of God with the saints—the language of silence. Dynamic silence is palpable, but mysterious; real, but elusive. It is a filled-up silence. Sam's spiritual director tells him often enough, "You'll wait through a lot of empty silence before you break through into filled-up silence. All the saints had to learn to wait like this in the same way."

"Why do I need to go through this?" Sam asked. "Because it's the only way God can convince you what the transforming power of prayer really is," responded his spiritual director. "God doesn't want to be entertained or impressed or convinced of anything. What God wants from you is your openness to love and love's power to change you from a busy animal into a friend of God. Remember what Jesus called his one commandment: 'abide in my love. . . . love one another as I have loved you' (John 15:10-12). It takes a lot of stripping away of false ideas about God and about love before we really learn the love that brought Jesus through death to new life. That's our life now." The love of God becomes experienced in faithful, loving silence.

What matters above all is that we show up and give God our time in prayer. Centering prayer or prayer following the principles of Ignatian spirituality are other examples of transforming prayer that help priests to establish a discipline of regular listening prayer in their lives. What we feel or experience is not what matters in prayer, but rather our firm intention to be with God who is the only one who can transform us. We seek to make ourselves ready for this promised divine grace.

SPIRITUAL DIRECTION

During their seminary days, priests were obliged to work with a spiritual director. However, the great majority of

The primary responsibility for ongoing formation belongs to priests themselves: "The priest himself, the individual priest . . . is the person primarily responsible in the Church for ongoing formation. Truly each priest has the duty, rooted in the Sacrament of Holy Orders, to be faithful to the gift God has given him and to respond to the call for daily conversion which comes with the gift itself." (*OFP* 51; cf. *PDV* §79)

priests abandon the practice of spiritual direction soon after leaving the seminary, despite the fact that the seminary's insistence on direction was meant to instill a lifelong habit. In the past, seminary professors were sometimes assigned to act as spiritual directors without very much training or clear signals about what was expected of them. Sometimes neither the spiritual director nor the one coming for direction was especially clear about just what this practice was meant to accomplish. What's going on here?

Spiritual direction is often called by other names, especially outside the context of religious life. It is called spiritual companioning, spiritual discernment, or spiritual conversation, as well as spiritual friendship. The adjective "spiritual" here refers explicitly to the Holy Spirit, whose guidance, healing, and energy both the director and the directee seek in their shared practice.

A good director is a good listener who hears both what is said and what is felt, what gets spoken and what's avoided. Quite often, in the process of finding themselves really listened to, priests dare to say to themselves in spiritual direction something that they have been feeling and aching about, but avoiding at the same time. They enter spiritual direction with the profound hope of discovering God's will through the director's listening and counsel.

Spiritual direction is a form of active and conversational prayer. The director serves a quasi-sacramental role by listening to what is deepest in the heart of the client and inviting honesty, freedom, and deep feeling out into the open. Sometimes a simple act of enabling pain to surface or probing where it seems evident that deep feelings lie, can open up a much needed flood of avoided issues.

> "There are specific means whereby this unifying and integrating pastoral love becomes more conscious and more accessible to priests. Spiritual direction, for example, is an extraordinarily useful means for retrieving the experience of ministry, the presence of the Lord, and the integrating-unifying directions that God gives through the ministry." (*OFP* 31)

Put more simply, spiritual direction allows us to speak from our heart to God through the skilled and patient listening of a helping minister. It is life-giving and healing to arrive at the point where we can say to ourselves and to God, as honestly as we know how, the truth about our joys and our anguish. We have nothing to hide and nothing to fear. We dare to tell the truth and live the truth in these moments—and we know better where we have to pay attention in the days to come. It is a way station on a journey. Each time we enter direction, we see more clearly where we're going and take heart to move on.

Spiritual direction is not therapy and not crisis counseling. A good spiritual director is trained to recognize self-destructive tendencies, clinical depression, and personality disorders, and will not attempt to treat or engage these. A trained clinical professional is needed for them. Direction is about spiritual growth, not problem solving. A good director will inquire about a priest's habits of prayer, his work habits, recreation and exercise, his social network, and his enthusiasms and successes. He will be attentive to the question of a human balance in the priest-client's life, reflecting the issues of human development that we examined earlier.

Relative to prayer, especially, the director will want to hear what's happening—especially in quiet prayer—as the priest grows in his experience of God. The director should be able to help explain what might be going on, where typical obstacles to growth may lie, and then encourage the priest to risk the pain of the darkness and silence that surround growth in prayer, if that is where the person is being led. If someone is having that kind of trouble, then he really needs this kind of help.

Each person is as different in spiritual personality as we are distinct in our physiognomy. God loves variety. Thomas Merton once wrote that many people never become saints because they spend their life trying to live out somebody else's agenda for holiness. Good spiritual direction will help a priest discover his true freedom and his real self—the self that God wants to see incarnated in the spiritual journey of his life. There is both joy and loneliness in the recognition of that reality. It is a joy to know that God loves the unrepeatable uniqueness that I am—my personality, my gifts, my achievements, and my prayer. It is lonely, however, to realize that at the deepest level of my person, where I am alone with God in the core of my being, I cannot count on someone else to show me the way. I have to respond to God for myself and let God lead me more deeply into the mystery of Christ.

Here again the dying and the rising of the paschal mystery is evident. I am being asked to die to my dependence on someone else's judgment, to my patterning of my life on another's gifts or achievements, even to my ability to plan out and control the unfolding of my spiritual life. There is dying in yielding my own preferences to God's mysterious providence for me. Yet this is exactly what is needed to rise into the new creation, the new life that Christ won for us. The new self, the real self, that God has destined us for is the self that draws life from the gifts of the Holy Spirit.

"Many poets are not poets for the same reason that many religious people are not saints: they never succeed in being themselves. They never get around to being the particular poet or the particular monk they are intended to be by God. They never become the person or the artist who is called for by all the circumstances of their individual lives." (Merton 1961, 98)

"Their conscience is people's most secret core, and their sanctuary. There they are alone with God whose voice echoes in their depths. By conscience, in a wonderful way, that law is made known which is fulfilled in the love of God and of one's neighbor." (GS §16)

It was always a good idea for a priest to have a spiritual director. It is close to obligatory today. With all the burdens, all the demands, all the temptations, and all the ambiguity that surround a priest's spiritual life, spiritual direction can be both a beacon through the dark confusion of an anxious life and a loving support in the midst of loneliness.

Sam fought the idea of spiritual direction for a long time. He was so busy that he just didn't think he had time for it. And the truth is: it is not easy for a parish priest to find helpful spiritual direction. Some retreat houses provide spiritual directors, but often they are some distance away. Sam was lucky. He found a fellow parish priest who had some experience doing spiritual direction. Now he considers this one of the most essential parts of his spiritual practice.

A spiritual director has to be someone serious about his or her own spiritual life. The director's role, as is clear from Sam's story, is to get out of the way of the Holy Spirit, but also, because of their common sense and their own experience, help the directee to hear what God is saying to them in their prayer and ministry. Clearly the U.S. Church needs priests to prepare themselves for this critical ministry.

Once a month Sam spends fifty minutes reviewing his life and exploring his prayer with his spiritual director's help. "Often I don't know exactly what I'm going to say even as I walk into my director's study. I always spend some time ahead thinking about what I will need to address. But pretty frequently, something much deeper and more urgent than I realized suddenly starts forming in my thoughts and tumbling out of my mouth," thinks Sam. "I am really grateful that I have Father Harry; he helps me to tell the truth about myself in a way that nobody else in my life does. It's a gift."

STEWARD OF THE MYSTERIES OF GOD

Sam enjoys leading his parish in the Eucharist, especially on Sunday morning. It is the moment when he is privileged to gather together the families and the individuals of the parish who assemble to hear God's revealing word and to give thanks for their lives and their blessings. Sam has learned by experience that he himself will enjoy the Sunday celebrations only to the degree that he prepares himself to preach with conviction and celebrate with enthusiasm. He knows that celebrating these liturgies can become mostly routine if he isn't careful.

His liturgical leadership of the parish is a lot of work. He has a vigil Mass on Saturday night and three Masses on Sunday—and most of the time he has no one to help him. Deacon Bill comes for one Mass on Sunday morning, usually at 9:30, and that adds a bit of solemnity. Bill shares in some of the ritual supervision of acolytes and other ministers. But Sam has to extend himself to hundreds of people, week after week, at all these Masses. At times that feels overwhelming. He knows that some priests of his diocese offer Mass in two or more parishes every weekend. He wonders how they deal with the expectations and the disappointment of the people.

Sam began his homily preparation on Monday by reading through the next Sunday's Lectionary readings. Several times in the course of the week he spent time thinking about what these readings mean for this community. On Wednesday nights Sam has a Scripture sharing group in the parish that prays over and discusses the Sunday readings with him. That kind of sharing of the Sunday readings always puts him well on the way to feeling he knows where his sermon should go on Sunday morning. By Sunday he is eager for his people to feel that God is speaking to them personally about their lives in this specific place. His shared prayer with parishioners helps him to feel confident about bringing the Gospel home to the parish.

Sam read an old Hassidic tale concerning an elderly rabbi who no longer presided over his synagogue, but who still came faithfully every week. When the reading from the prophet began with the words, "God spoke to his people and said . . . ," the old man would mumble in astonishment: "God has spoken to his people. . . . God has spoken to his people. . . . Think of that!" Sam considers this story as an example of an important truth: "Do we even realize what we are doing here?"

Sam thinks, "How can I help these folks realize that God really speaks to them when the Scriptures are read in the Mass? How can I help them understand that their own lives can become an act of obedience to what they hear in God's Word? How can my preaching prepare them for this mystery?"

In a way everything flows from there. The gifts we bring are our response to God's Word calling us to

"The homily is liturgy. Its words are the words of the liturgy as much as the prayers of the presider or the songs of the assembly. We are told time and again that faithful Catholics want good preaching and homilists who develop and hone their skills. . . . Take to heart the germ of an idea in *Fulfilled in Your Hearing:* that homilists meet regularly with members of the assembly to read and ponder the Sunday Scriptures." (*GFT* §§157, 159)

discipleship—we give ourselves through the symbol of our offerings. The thanksgiving we lift up is our offering to God of the risen Christ, head and members, as a living sacrifice of praise. Our communion is a sharing in the new life of the risen Christ. And then, as a people who have been taught and nourished, we are sent forth. Sometimes at the dismissal Sam says, "Go, the Mass is ended and your new life has begun." The gathered believers are now scattered to be apostles.

Sam saw a sign posted in the exit ramp of the parking lot at a nearby Evangelical Church: "You are Entering Mission Territory." Just right! The priestly life of his priestly people is mostly lived "out there." For so many years, people failed to understand that the Mass was their celebration, that the offering was of their lives, and that the gift of the Lord's Body and Blood was food for an apostolic journey—the journey of their own life and integrity. The entire experience of the sacrament means so much more to Sam when he remembers that he is leading them as one of them.

St. Augustine used to say to his people: "To you I am the bishop, with you I am a Christian" (Sermon 340.1; cited in *LG* §32). Sam knows that this is the meaning of his ministerial priesthood too: "With you I am a Christian; and for you I am your priest. I will preach and bless and try to lead as your servant and your friend." He knows that he must pray for them also when they have returned home. A pastor prays for his people.

THE LITURGY OF THE HOURS

Like many other priests, Sam has had his ups and downs with the breviary. He remembers being taught in the seminary that the breviary was a serious obligation that he was required to undertake, but he didn't take too readily to praying the psalms at first. However, on a clergy renewal day, a liturgist presented some helpful ideas that were new to him. The fundamental structure of the breviary is a pattern to sanctify the hours of the day. The Liturgy of the Hours grew out of the practice of monasteries to mark the times of the day with formulas of psalms, readings, and prayers. The two great hours, Morning Prayer and Evening Prayer, orient the day's activities: setting up the work of the day in a context of praise and closing down the activities of the day with thanksgiving.

Here too, as with personal and private prayer, Sam is learning that this prayer is not so much about the message of the words as about the spirit of the Divine Office. The goal of the prayer is not so much to follow and think about every single word as to join the Church in prayer and, with the Church, to join Christ in his eternal priestly prayer in the presence of the Father. The divine office requires an act of creative imagination in order to see yourself joined to others throughout the world who praise and intercede—along with and in the name of the risen Christ.

Sam was also reminded on the clergy day that the ordination rite commissioned him to celebrate the Divine Office as a work of intercession on behalf of the people of God. Like Moses beseeching God for mercy after the sin of the golden calf, Sam begs God to understand his people's forgetfulness, failures, and weakness, and to help them in their deepest needs. This is easier to do when he is aware of those sick in the hospital, of couples struggling to stay together, of kids in trouble with drugs and gangs, and of the anguish of fellow priests on the ropes because of overwork or discouragement.

The passage of *Sacrosanctum Concilium* (The Constitution on the Sacred Liturgy) advocating sharing the Divine Office with the laity had been brought to Sam's attention in the seminary. It reads:

[W]hen this wonderful song of praise is correctly celebrated by priests and others deputed for this purpose by the Church's ordinance, or by the faithful praying together with a priest in an approved form, then it is truly the voice of the bride herself addressed to her bridegroom. And what is more, it is the prayer which Christ himself together with his body addresses to the Father. (SC §83)

Sam celebrates Sunday Evening Prayer in church at 7:15 P.M. and each week more of his people are coming. For some of them, this is a moment of deep significance and spiritual refreshment. He wishes everyone in the parish would have the experience of Sunday Evening Prayer at some point. The light of the paschal candle in the gathering darkness really centers everyone present on Christ who is the Light of the World. He wonders when his lay associates will be able to effectively preside some of the time—to assure this ministry of prayer and to take that responsibility off his shoulders. They can do it, he's sure; but it will require careful formation. (One more thing to do!)

"Jesus Christ, high priest of the new and eternal covenant, taking human nature, introduced into this earthly exile that hymn which is sung throughout all ages in the realms above. He joins the entire community of humankind to himself, associating it with himself in singing his divine song of praise. For it is through his church itself that he continues this priestly work." (SC §83)

"In some places the Divine Office has already taken on a broader dimension as the Prayer of the Church or the Prayer of Christians instead of being simply 'the priest's prayer.' The Divine Office as the prayer of a small community led by the priest not only accords with the intent of the Church in revising the breviary, as the Roman document on the Liturgy of the Hours brings out, but actually confirms the intuition of many priests who see this form as foundational for their own personal prayer lives and their prayer with others." (SR 51)

Sam still must make a conscious effort to connect praying the breviary with the stuff of everyday life. Often his Morning Prayer is filled with images from the headlines—the Middle East; the terrorist threat; famine and poverty; homeless adults, children, families: the painful agenda of a conflicted world struggling for unity and peace and survival. "Lord, I hand them all over to you," thinks Sam as the lamentations of the psalms or the promises of the prophets pass beneath his glance. "Mercy!"

His Evening Prayer is more like rest and thanksgiving. A retreat master once suggested that he read the first reading of the Mass in the morning and the Gospel of the Mass at Evening Prayer in place of the "little chapter," and he often does this. It reminds him of the link between his personal devotions and his parish community, and that is another motivation to keep him at it.

Sam knows that many priests don't pray the breviary. Some choose other prayers from other prayer books. Some just lose interest. Sam now understands more clearly that his priesthood is not uniquely cultic but comprehensive, and it includes a call to engage in this work of praise and intercession on behalf of his people.

"Lord, help me find rest and strength in this like Jesus did," Sam prays. "Help me figure out how to do this prayer of intercession. Give me a generous heart."

For many priests, the ministry is a much more up and down roller coaster ride than what we see here. Sam's story illustrates the disciplines that can stabilize a priest's difficult life, although they require consistent focus and practice. Wherever a priest finds himself, however, he can be sure of Christ's tender mercy and on-going forgiveness. To every priest Christ says, "Come to me, all you that are weary and carrying heavy burdens, and I will give you rest" (Matt 11:28).

Sam's life has become a paschal journey. Through his pastoral leadership and ministry, his listening and reflection, his community prayer and his private prayer he has become a servant leader who is a true disciple of Jesus. He is grateful for his many priestly roles and he is attentive to his own need for growth and peace in his life. He really believes that God is at work in him and through him. He finds strength in friendship and power in obedience. He is called to be one with Christ, and he is happy to answer "Yes" with his life.

"The question to be asked by each priest at this point…is the following: What does all this mean to me? How do I put it all together and personally integrate it, personally appropriate it in my life? How do I make the ideal described in these pages real for me? How do I assimilate the death and resurrection of Christ and live that mystery? In a word, how am I transformed into Christ?" (SR 57)

Agenda for Personal and Group Reflection

QUESTIONS FOR THE INDIVIDUAL PRIEST

1. How am I doing on consistency? Am I living one life or two?

2. Do I have a place or space that's dedicated to personal prayer? If not, can I think of one that's right for that?

3. How are my listening skills? Do I enjoy staff meetings and other parish meetings? Do I need help to do better? How can I find that out?

4. Do I have a spiritual director? A regular confessor? Do I feel like I need help and encouragement to continue to grow in the spiritual life?

5. Do I work on my Sunday preaching throughout the preceding week? Do I ever get together with staff members or parishioners to read and study the readings of Sunday in preparation for celebrating and preaching?

6. What other challenging questions have I taken away from reading this chapter on spiritual practices?

QUESTIONS FOR GROUP DISCUSSION

1. Has the diocese offered lectures or workshops on growth in personal prayer to the priests in recent years? Do we perhaps need one now?

2. How are our skills for listening to one another in this gathering (support group, deanery meeting, diocesan workshop)? Does everyone check in, speak up, listen, and reflect? Does each person get a chance to count for something?

3. Does the diocese provide a roster of names of priests and others who are skilled in spiritual direction for priests? Can the religious men and women of the diocese be encouraged to provide skilled spiritual directors for priests?

4. How do we prepare for preaching? What are our best resources, methods, and practices?

5. What other questions arise out of this reflection on priestly spiritual practices?

Chapter Seven

A Fresh Call to Renewal

At the conclusion of this review of the spirituality of U.S. Catholic priests at the start of the third millennium, it is appropriate to note that, all things considered, priests here are remarkably content. The *Los Angeles Times* conducted a national survey of 1,854 diocesan and religious priests in eighty dioceses in the weeks following the Catholic Bishops' June 2002 meeting in Dallas. Their analysis reveals that priests are happy in their chosen life, even though they feel embattled by negative media attention. Ninety-one percent said that they are very (70%) or somewhat (21%) satisfied with the way their life as priests is going. Sixty percent said that their life in the priesthood had turned out better than they had expected, and more than 70 percent said that they would definitely make the same choice again—along with 20 percent who said that they would probably do so (*Los Angeles Times,* 20 October 2002).

The *Los Angeles Times* data is supported by Hoge and Wenger's recent study of Catholic priests that shows that satisfaction with priesthood has increased in recent decades. According to this research, 94 percent of priests are either "very happy" (45%) or "pretty happy" (49%) with their life as priests. Hoge and Wenger's data comes from 2001, before the priests' sex abuse crisis, so we cannot tell what impact those events have had upon the study's respondents. But the *Los Angles Times* survey was calculated to test for exactly that impact, and it shows the same positive reading of priests' satisfaction. We have to conclude that Catholic priests are men who are happy in their calling and fulfilled in their ministry.

At the same time, Hoge and Wenger's research indicates clear signs of generational and ideological shifts

81

among priests. Their research shows a clear movement by recent priests toward rejection of post-Vatican attitudes about the Church and a preference for pre-Vatican teachings. But deeper than their differences about attitudes concerning authority and priestly identity, we hope, is the solidarity of the presbyterate as the unified corps of those ordained to assist bishops in their pastoral ministry. We dare to hope that this document will provide an occasion for the recently ordained to dialogue with the older priests of the diocese, and for all of them to identify and claim some common ground. What we all have in common by our faith and our call to the service of the Gospel is far more significant than what divides us in attitudes and ideas.

Despite the general positive health of American priests, we are nonetheless in a period of grave concern. Over the past forty years, 1.8 percent of U.S. Catholic priests have been accused of perpetrating some act of sexual abuse according to a sensationalized news report of the *New York Times* (12 January 2003). The *New York Times* claims 1,205 abusing priests and 4,268 victims. Those facts, if generally accurate, are horrifying. Equally disturbing is the insatiable appetite of the *New York Times* and its affiliated newspapers to humiliate the Roman Catholic Church on the basis of this scandal. Much of the Church's credibility and moral capital has been squandered, especially by the refusal of certain bishops to be accountable for their reassignment of perpetrators. We will carry this wound with us for a long time to come.

CAUSE FOR CELEBRATION

However, the publication of this present study was prompted by the thirtieth anniversary of *The Spiritual Renewal of the American Priesthood,* and an anniversary is a time for celebration. So we should observe our reasons to rejoice.

The vitality and creativity of pastors in the U.S. Church over the forty years since Vatican II is cause for thanksgiving. Priests ordained in the 1950s and 1960s have spent their entire priestly life adjusting to cultural, theological, and liturgical change. This generation especially made the introduction of the council's reforms smooth sailing for American Catholics. But the priests who have followed after them have also had to deal with serious challenges, including growing numbers, growing diversity, and growing demands for new ministries.

The resilience and generosity of American priests is amazing. The median age of priests is now 60. This means, among other things, that half of the priests in the U.S. have graciously responded many times to changes in liturgy, pastoral trends, styles of episcopal leadership, and people's attitudes. The perseverance of so many priests in their late 60s, 70s, and even 80s in parish ministry is a tribute to lives completely dedicated to the common good of Christ's Church.

We celebrate as well the continued relevance and helpfulness of the spiritual doctrine of *The Spiritual Renewal of the American Priesthood*. The doctrine of the paschal mystery of Christ is expressed with somewhat different emphasis in these pages, but it remains the same doctrinal key that opens up the meaning of priestly life.

We should note that both the 1973 study and this present one have concentrated principally on diocesan priests and parish leadership. However, slightly less than one-third of U.S. priests are clerical religious. For them, the charism of their religious institute is the chief governing norm for their mission and ministry. It is important that religious priests perform ministries that are genuinely coherent with the charism of their order, institute, or congregation. Care will be needed not to co-opt their energies for parish supply, if parish ministry is not really their calling. Further, good diocesan pastoral planning will be interested in exploring how religious institutes may most effectively serve the mission of the diocese. Paramount pastoral concerns, like adult faith formation, pastoral training for lay ecclesial ministers, spiritual direction for priests, and evangelization, may be exactly what these groups of religious were founded to do for the Church. It will be important to take advantage of these charisms and employ them judiciously.

AN APPEAL

At the start of this study, we noted that this little book is intended as a "study document" whose aim is to start a conversation. We are asking great generosity of American bishops and priests to follow through and make sure that they meet, talk, air their differences, and seek unity on the basis of deeper mutual understanding.

One of the theological themes developed here, posed by the council documents and the *Catechism,* is the ministerial priesthood as an office at the service of the common priesthood. In light of that theme, it should be noted that the lay faithful are at present a sort of sleeping giant, who do not generally understand their role as apostles in the "evangelization of culture" (to use a phrase coined by Pope Paul VI and clearly loved by Pope John Paul II). As we consider our own solidarity in ordained ministry, we should keep in mind the potential transforming presence of the faithful in the world.

All the faithful are called to holiness. Their awakening to this vocation will depend upon our responding to the importance of our role as prophets—through solid Christian preaching, persevering adult faith formation, and leadership in the ministry of justice. As noted above, this is synergy. We will find our pastoral soul precisely in addressing the needs of the common priesthood for prophetic leadership.

We began with Paul's First Letter to the Corinthians. With him, we recognize that we too have been called to be stewards of the mysteries of God. This stewardship requires of us that we live the mystery of Christ as the pattern for our own ministry and self-giving. It implies a lifelong effort to immerse ourselves more deeply into the mysteries of divine revelation and the practices of the spiritual life. It also presupposes that we will commit ourselves to our priesthood, that is our life's work and its joy, in company with confreres who likewise seek the Lord above all else.

This study is a fresh call to renewal for American priests. Never before has our ministry been more critical or the potential for our effectiveness greater. Serving as a priest—including the acceptance of the comprehensive complex of roles that shape our ministry today—is both difficult and immeasurably rewarding. We must help one another to remember who we are and the dignity and the destiny that is ours. Let us think of ourselves in this way: as servants of Christ and stewards of the mysteries of God.

Bibliography

Barron, Robert E. "Priest as Bearer of the Mystery." In *Priesthood in the Modern World,* edited by Karen Sue Smith, 101–9. Franklin, Wis.: Sheed & Ward, 1999.

Blanchette, Melvin C. *A Guide for the Rekindling of Priestly Life and Ministry.* Baltimore, Md.: St. Mary's Seminary and University, 1991.

Bonvin, Bernard. *Dieu silence, Dieu présence.* Paris: Éditions du Cerf, 2000.

Brown, Raymond E. "An Example: Rethinking the Priesthood Biblically for All." In *The Critical Meaning of the Bible,* 96–106. New York: Paulist Press, 1981.

———. "The Challenge of the Three Priesthoods." *The Catholic Mind* 78 (March 1980) 11–20.

———. *Priest and Bishop: Biblical Reflections.* New York: Paulist Press, 1970.

Catechism of the Catholic Church. Washington, D.C.: United States Catholic Conference, 1994.

Catholic Priest in the United States, The: Sociological Investigations. Washington, D.C.: United States Catholic Conference, 1972.

Celibacy for the Kingdom: Theological Reflections and Practical Perspectives. Baltimore, Md.: St. Mary's Seminary and University, 1990.

D'Antonio, William V., et al., eds. *American Catholics: Gender, Generation, and Commitment.* Walnut Creek, Calif.: AltaMira Press, 2001.

———. *Laity: American and Catholic: Transforming the Church.* Kansas City, Mo.: Sheed & Ward, 1996.

Delbrêl, Madeleine. *La Joie de croire.* Paris: Éditions du Seuil, 1980.

Dulles, Avery. *The Priestly Office: A Theological Reflection.* New York: Paulist Press, 1997.

Ellis, John Tracy, ed. *The Catholic Priest in the United States: Historical Investigations.* Collegeville, Minn.: Saint John's University Press, 1971.

Flannery, Austin. *Vatican II: Constitutions, Decrees, Declarations.* Rev. translation. Northport, N.Y.: Costello, 1996.

Friedl, Francis P., and Rex Reynolds, eds. *Extraordinary Lives: Thirty-Four Priests Tell Their Stories.* Notre Dame, Ind.: Ave Maria Press, 1997.

Goergen, Donald J., and Ann Garrido, eds. *The Theology of Priesthood.* Collegeville, Minn.: The Liturgical Press, 2000.

Greeley, Andrew M. "The Times and Sexual Abuse by Priests." *America,* 10 February 2003, 17.

Hennessy, Paul K., ed. *A Concert of Charisms: Ordained Ministry in Religious Life.* New York: Paulist Press, 1997.

Himes, Michael J. "Making Priesthood Possible: Who Does What and Why?" In Karen Sue Smith, ed., *Priesthood in the Modern World,* 39–49. Franklin, Wisc.: Sheed & Ward, 1999.

Hoge, Dean R. *The First Five Years of the Priesthood: A Study of Newly Ordained Catholic Priests.* Collegeville, Minn.: The Liturgical Press, 2002.

———. *The Future of Catholic Leadership: Responses to the Priest Shortage.* Kansas City: Sheed & Ward, 1987.

Hoge, Dean R., et al. *Young Adult Catholics: Religion in the Culture of Crisis.* Notre Dame, Ind.: University of Notre Dame Press, 2001.

Hoge, Dean R., and Jacqueline E. Wenger. *Evolving Visions of the Priesthood: Changes from Vatican II to the Turn of the New Century.* Collegeville, Minn.: Liturgical Press, 2003.

Holy Spirit, Lord and Giver of Life, The. Prepared by the Theological-Historical Commission for The Great Jubilee of the Year 2000. New York: Crossroad, 1997.

Johann, Robert O. *Building the Human.* New York: Herder and Herder, 1968.

Kennedy, Eugene C., and Victor J. Heckler, eds. *The Catholic Priest in the United States: Psychological Investigations.* Washington, D.C.: United States Catholic Conference, 1972.

Kunkel, Thomas. *Enormous Prayers: A Journey into the Priesthood.* Boulder, Colo.: Westview Press, 1998.

Mahony, Roger Michael. *Gather Faithfully Together: Guide for Sunday Mass.* Chicago, Ill.: Liturgy Training Publications, 1997.

Merton, Thomas. *New Seeds of Contemplation.* New York: New Directions, 1961.

Murnion, Philip J. "Common Ground, Holy Ground: A Ministry of Grace and Communion." In Karen Sue Smith, ed., *Priesthood in the Modern World,* 1–17. Franklin, Wis.: Sheed & Ward, 1999.

―――. "Priest: Beyond Employee, To Minister of the Sacred." *National Catholic Reporter,* 27 September 2002, 10–11.

Murnion, Philip J., and David DeLambo. *Parishes and Parish Ministers: A Study of Parish Lay Ministry.* New York: National Pastoral Life Center, 1999.

Nouwen, Henri J. M. *The Wounded Healer: Ministry in Contemporary Society.* Garden City, N.Y.: Doubleday, 1979.

Philibert, Paul. "Cross-Referencing Pastoral Challenges of the First and 21st Centuries." *Origins* 31 (2001) 341–46.

"Poll Analysis: Priests Say Catholic Church Facing Biggest Crisis of the Century." *Los Angeles Times,* 20 October 2002. http://www.latimes.com/news/custom/timespoll/la-timespollpriests.

Priestless Parishes: Priests' Perspective. Chicago, Ill.: National Federation of Priests' Councils, 1991.

Putnam, Robert D. *Bowling Alone: The Collapse and Revival of American Community.* New York: Simon and Schuster, 2000.

Quartier, Neal E. "Survival Manual for Parish Priests." In Karen Sue Smith, ed., *Priesthood in the Modern World,* 77–83. Franklin, Wis.: Sheed & Ward, 1999.

Schoenherr, Richard A. and Lawrence A. Young. *Full Pews and Empty Altars: Demographics of the Priest Shortage in United States Catholic Dioceses.* Madison, Wis.: University of Wisconsin Press, 1993.

Schwartz, Robert M. *Servant Leaders of the People of God: An Ecclesial Spirituality for American Priests.* New York: Paulist Press, 1989.

Together in God's Service: Toward a Theology of Ecclesial Lay Ministry. Washington, D.C.: United States Catholic Conference, 1998.

Walsh, James, et al. *Grace Under Pressure: What Gives Life to American Priests: A Study of Effective Priests Ordained Ten to Thirty Years.* Washington, D.C.: National Catholic Educational Association, 1995.

Wood, Susan K. *Sacramental Orders.* Lex Orandi series. Collegeville, Minn.: The Liturgical Press, 2000.